I CAME AS A STRANGER

I CAME AS A STRANGER

The Underground Railroad

BRYAN PRINCE

Tundra Books

Published in Canada by Tundra Books,
481 University Avenue, Toronto, Ontario M5G 2E9

Published in the United States by Tundra Books of Northern New York,
P.O. Box 1030, Plattsburgh, New York 12901

Library of Congress Control Number: 2003114597

National Library of Canada Cataloguing in Publication

Prince, Bryan, 1952-
    I came as a stranger : the Underground Railroad / Bryan Prince.

Includes bibliographical references and index.
ISBN 0-88776-667-6

    1. Fugitive slaves – Canada – Juvenile literature. 2. Blacks – Canada – History – Juvenile literature. 3. Underground railroad – Juvenile literature. 4. Black Canadians – History – Juvenile literature. I. Title.

FC106.B6P76 2004   J971'.00496   C2003-906550-2

We acknowledge the financial support of the Government of Canada through the Book Publishing Industry Development Program (BPIDP) and that of the Government of Ontario through the Ontario Media Development Corporation's Ontario Book Initiative. We further acknowledge the support of the Canada Council for the Arts and the Ontario Arts Council for our publishing program.

Design: Cindy Reichle

Printed and bound in Canada

1 2 3 4 5 6   09 08 07 06 05 04

This photo is one of my all-time personal favorites. To me it speaks of many things: the promise and future of newly freed people; the variety of hues of skin color that was a reality of many slave families; and the thousands of unidentified blacks who sought freedom in Canada, whose stories we will never know.

This book is dedicated to all those colleagues and friends scattered across the Province of Ontario who have given so much of themselves to research, to preserve, and to share the history of those who participated in what has come to be known as the Underground Railroad. Although the tales that follow are only the tiniest tip of the iceberg, they are a tribute to you who have worked so hard to reveal what has for so long been submerged. It is my sincerest hope that *I Came As a Stranger* will, in a small way, help inspire the interest of the public, and draw attention to your efforts and to the stories you tell.

Contents

INTRODUCTION

There is a growing fascination across North America with the story of the "Underground Railroad" – the informal network of daring people and safe refuges, in both the United States and Canada, that helped thousands of fugitives escape the evils of slavery. In the United States, academic institutions, historians, genealogists, and media outlets have for years been sharing the American side of the story with an increasingly enthusiastic audience. Less well known, but an essential part of the story, is the role that Ontario – once known as Upper Canada, then as Canada West – played in this drama. Scattered across the province are individuals, museums, churches, and historical societies striving to conserve and present this enthralling tale. Numerous National Historic designations assigned within the past decade testify to the value Canada places on the struggles and triumphs of the people who followed the North Star to freedom. Thousands visit these historic sites annually, vastly more thousands make contact by phone or by mail, or visit the

It's one thing to hear about captured Africans being marched away to slavery in a distant continent. But when you have before you the actual shackles, chains, and handcuffs that were locked onto human bodies, it's not just a story any more.

websites, and many groups invite Underground Railroad historians to address their members. Perhaps most important, the story of the Underground Railroad is now taught in many classrooms across the continent, ensuring that future generations will not forget the importance of those tumultuous years.

Some of the photographs that appear on the following pages can be found in the museums and heritage sites listed at the end of the book, where there is also a map of their locations.

The stories celebrated in these historic sites are many; our pages here are few. We hope you will come and visit the sites themselves, for a closer experience of these remarkable people, and the desperate times in which they lived. For more information, see the last chapter, "Tracing Their Steps Today."

This lively quilt, made by Marion Lyons for the Chatham-Kent Black Historical Society, captures some memorable images: upper left, a woman slaving in the cotton fields of the south; bottom left, a family reaching the safety of Canada. At the time Canada was still a British possession, so the flag shown is Britain's Union Jack.

1

HUMAN CARGO, HUMAN WARES

"wanted, to purchase a negro girl,
from seven to twelve years of age . . ."

The story of the Underground Railroad is a chapter in a much larger story. That story began in Africa, where people were captured, traded, and sold. It continued on board ships that carried them across the Atlantic Ocean, in a nightmare trip known as the Middle Passage. Next, the victims – those fortunate enough to survive the voyage – found themselves driven onto auction blocks, and sold to the highest bidder. In the fields and businesses and homes of their new masters, they would labor and suffer and die as slaves. Their children would inherit their slavery and their pain, which would be passed down through the generations.

The Atlantic slave trade began around the early 1500s, not long after Christopher Columbus arrived in the New World. Many European countries, including Portugal, Spain, the Netherlands, England, and France, participated. Millions of Africans were captured, usually by other Africans, and forced to march to holding pens on the coast until they could be loaded

Captured Africans were bound and chained together, and driven like cattle to the sea. Then they were penned up – often in sweltering heat, perhaps with no water – until ships came to take them away. Some died before the ships even got there. Imagine the terror that must have spread through African villages whenever word went round that the slave-hunters were back.

onto sailing ships. Some of these unlucky people had been captured by their enemies, as prisoners of war. Others had been sentenced to slavery as punishment for crimes – even crimes as minor as stealing a tobacco pipe. Yet others were tricked into boarding the ship, believing that they were going on business; or were fooled into sending their children to Europe "to be educated." Sometimes children were sold by their own parents, as payment for debt.

Historians estimate that, one way or another, between thirteen and fifteen million Africans were boarded onto slave ships for the trip across the ocean. Of that number, perhaps only ten million survived.

The largest number of slaves were shipped to the Caribbean islands of the West Indies. Many were put to work in the sugarcane fields, helping produce sugar for the European market. While they were making their owners rich, the slaves were also becoming conditioned to the work and the climate. Those who survived could then be resold to more lucrative markets, particularly in the American south. Almost three and a half million slaves were sent to Brazil, in South America. Nearly two million were delivered directly to the North American continent, and others arrived there via the Caribbean.

Slavery Elsewhere

Although this book talks about slavery as part of the history of the Western hemisphere, slavery has played a role in history around the world. Wherever people have been enslaved, they have longed to escape, and other people – people of conscience – have lent their assistance, or at least their sympathies, to aid in that escape. "Underground Railroads" would develop, in different forms, in many of those places – in the ancient biblical time of Moses and the Egyptian pharaohs, for example.

Although many people think of slavery as part of American history, it was also very much a part of early Canadian history, from the Maritimes to the coast of the Pacific. Records show that, as early as 1501, a Portuguese explorer enslaved fifty native Canadian men and women. In 1632, a "Negro" boy, Oliver Le Jeune, is mentioned in Jesuit documents; he may have been the first African to be transported and sold into Canada. A brief but touching account of his life appears in *The Blacks in Canada: A History*, by the late Robin Winks. At about six years of age he was taken from Madagascar by the English. After traveling to England, he came with his new masters to New France (now

Slave ships were overloaded with their human cargo, and contagious diseases spread quickly. Captives who were dying or dead were tossed over the side. After the British outlawed slavery, some captains would drown their captives when they spotted a British ship, rather than be caught with illegal cargo.

Quebec) and was sold to a French clerk. Shortly thereafter, he was given to a person who seems to have been kindhearted. Oliver helped tend to his owner's family of ten children, and – unlike most slaves, who were kept illiterate – was allowed to be educated by a Jesuit (Catholic priest) teacher. He was also allowed to be baptized, and to take a family name; he chose "Le Jeune," his teacher's surname. Oliver died at about age thirty, apparently as a free person. We don't know how he was able to regain his freedom.

Slavery was very common in New France. Following the French surrender to the British in 1760, when French territories in Canada became British possessions, the French governor of Canada, the Marquis de Vaudreuil, described the liberal terms of surrender he had accepted: the French inhabitants would be allowed to keep their household goods and furs, and to continue to practice their religion. He added: "They keep their Negro or Panis [native] slaves but are obliged to give back those taken from the English." It seems that neither the English nor the French commanders minded the custom of slavery, as long as neither side could take away the other side's slaves.

For almost two centuries, both blacks and natives continued to work as slaves in Canada. They served as domestics and field hands, worked in the fur trade, and performed many other duties. Matthew Dolsen, who was of European descent, owned a tavern near present-day Chatham, Ontario, and had among his slaves a Panis woman who had been stolen as a child by members of the Chippewa tribe. His native neighbor, Sally Ainse, owned "Negro" slaves.

Even whites occasionally became slaves. Margaret Kleine was "adopted" as a slave by native chief Joseph Brant after her family was killed in the Mohawk Valley of New York. Brant later moved to what is now Brantford, Ontario, and brought his slaves with him. Margaret Kleine had better luck than most slaves – she married Jean Baptiste Rousseau, who helped to found the town of Ancaster – but her early experiences left a lasting mark, and so soured her disposition that she became known for being incapable of any acts of kindness.

Another young white girl, from a prominent family in Pennsylvania, was captured prior to August of 1782 – while the British and the Americans were still at war – and made a slave by a band of native raiders. Her name was Sarah Cole and she was ten years old. Sarah was sold to a prominent man near Kingston, Ontario, but when this came to the attention of the Canadian authorities they were outraged, stating that "national honor" was at stake. They threatened to make the owner forfeit the money he had paid for the girl and "if possible to punish and make him an

When slaves were sold at auction, buyers inspected them as if they were livestock, checking their hands, their feet, their teeth. Those being sold might be ordered to look more eager and energetic than they felt.

example to prevent such inhuman conduct for the Future." In the end, they purchased Sarah for the equivalent of $42.50 and a string of wampum (beads) and returned her to the American colonies, with other prisoners of war.

Stories such as Sarah's and Margaret's are poignant but rare. Overwhelming in their number are the stories of the darker-hued children whose bondage did not arouse public indignation – children such as the boy and girl slaves of William Jarvis, of York (now Toronto), who got little sympathy from the Canadian court in 1811. Accused of running away and stealing, the boy was packed off to jail and the girl was returned to the mercy of their master. National honor, it seems, was not involved.

The common image of slaves is of adults, strong-bodied men and women who were able to toil in the houses and the fields. For example, a *Niagara Herald* newspaper advertisement placed by the Widow Clement offered to sell a man and a woman who "have been bred to the business of the farm." The *York Gazette and Oracle* of February 19, 1806, advertised "Peggy, age forty, who two years before had absented herself without leave" and said Peggy's skills had been learned as a house-slave; she was touted as being a "tolerable washerwoman" who could also make soap and candles. Many other advertisements reinforced this image of experienced, capable grownups.

However, the reality is that slaves came in all ages. We are left to wonder what young life may have been sold to W. and J. Crooks, of West Niagara, who advertised in the October 11, 1791 *Gazette*, in chilling commercial jargon, "wanted, to purchase a negro girl, from seven to twelve years of age, of good disposition. For fuller particulars apply to the subscribers. . . ."

2

Oppression and Injustice

". . . my mistress, was a barbarous creature."

As more and more people were shipped to North America and bought as slaves, providing cheap labor for plantations, homesteads, and businesses, slave-owners could not be unaware of the misery around them.

Some slaves tried to escape, although it was terribly difficult; they didn't know the land, they weren't allowed to see maps or discuss routes, and any dark-skinned person traveling without an owner was suspected of being a runaway.

Newspapers carried stern warnings about harboring fugitives. In 1806, Peter Russell of York advised readers against aiding Peggy: "the public are hereby cautioned from employing or harbouring her without the owner's leave. Whoever will do so after this notice may expect to be treated as the law directs." Charles Field of Niagara (now Niagara-on-the-Lake) was even more direct: "All persons are forbidden harbouring, employing or concealing my Indian Slave Sal, as I am determined to prosecute any offender to the extremity of the law and persons who may suffer

Ran away from the subscriber a few
weeks ago,

A Negro Wench,

named SUE :—this is therefore to fore-
warn all manner of persons from harboring said wench under the penalties of
the laws.

JAMES CLARK, senior.

Niagara, August 17, 1795.

*This advertisement – with "ſ" replacing "s" in the style of the time –
appeared in the* Upper Canada Gazette *on August 19, 1795.*

her to remain in or upon their premises for the space of half an
hour, without my consent will be taken as offending and dealt
with accordingly."

Advertisements like these suggest that, even before slavery
was abolished in Canada, some people may have been working
together to help runaway slaves, in an early version of the
Underground Railroad.

Other slaves rebelled against overwork, miserable living conditions, and general cruelty. Worst of all was the possibility of
being separated from their loved ones. Many slave-owners
thought nothing of selling a husband away from his wife, or
selling parents away from their children. Families might be split
up as punishment, or simply to make a profit.

Sometimes a family was wrenched apart when an owner
died. For example, Antoine Louis Descompte *dit* Labadie, a
wealthy merchant near Sandwich (now part of Windsor),
Ontario, owned many slaves. In his will, dated May 26, 1806, he

Unspeakable devices were invented to control or punish slaves. The bizarre collar was meant to hinder the wearer if he tried to run through forested areas, as it would catch on branches and undergrowth. With the steel rod running from the collar to his feet, he could not sit or bend over. The pierced metal gag prevented the wearer from eating or drinking, and kept him silent, barely letting him breathe. The shackles are small ones, designed to fit the slim ankles of children.

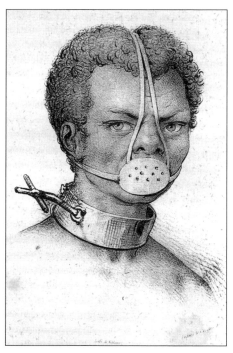

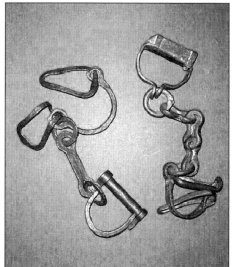

allowed his wife whichever two of his slaves she might select. All his other slaves were to be sold, and the proceeds divided among his wife and their nine children.

Surrounded and outnumbered by their own "possessions," many owners grew fearful of uprisings. Slaves were watched suspiciously, and any who seemed less than obedient were treated harshly. Some owners beat their slaves as a matter of course, to keep them in check.

John Baker, from Cornwall, Ontario, told his family's story in a Toronto newspaper two years before his death in 1871. His great-grandfather, Cato, had been captured in Africa and had become the slave of a man in Newark, New Jersey. Cato's granddaughter, Dorine, had been the property of a captain in the British army during the American Revolution. After the British lost the war, his was one of many Loyalist families who moved to Canada, first to Montreal, and later to Gray's Creek, three miles (5 km) from Cornwall. Before leaving Montreal, Dorine had married a Dutch man named Baker. But the fact that her husband was free and white did not matter. Because Dorine was a slave, the children born to her marriage were also slaves. John Baker was Dorine's youngest son.

In the newspaper interview, John Baker said that his first owner, Colonel Gray, was very strict and harsh with his slaves. John's older brother Simon received more humane treatment when he became the body servant of Colonel Gray's son, and was made to dress in a grand style with a beaver hat and a gold chain. However, before that, the colonel made them "wear deerskin shirts and deerskin jackets, and gave us many a flogging. At these times he would pull off my jacket, and the rawhide [whip] would fly around my shoulders very fast."

Any slave who was accused of breaking the law could expect no pity. Josiah Cutten, who had spent a lifetime in slavery for several owners in Massachusetts, Quebec, Michigan, and

Ontario, faced the wrath of a Canadian court in 1791, when he was charged with breaking into a shop and stealing some goods. While awaiting trial he was sold yet again, to someone who no doubt speculated that Cutten's penalty would be a return to slavery – the ultimate life sentence. If that was the case, the new owner was mistaken. Josiah Cutten was found guilty. In passing sentence, the judge compared him to a wild beast, adding, "This crime is so much more atrocious and alarming to society as it is committed by night when the world is at repose. . . ." Cutten was hanged at the gallows at Sandwich, the first person in Upper Canada (Ontario) to be legally hanged.

The Sandwich gallows were soon replaced by something even more diabolical. A few years later, two Chatham men – one black and one white – were hung by a gibbet, a metal frame that enclosed the lynched person. The corpses were displayed along a main road, for all passersby to see, and remained there as they decomposed. The sight and the odor became so offensive that one night some unidentified person (presumed by many to be the sheriff) cut the bodies and the gibbets down, and disposed of them. They were not rediscovered until over fifty years later, when they were unearthed in a gravel pit.

Legal documents and newspapers are among the few sources we have now to help us understand what it was like in those pioneer times, when slavery was, for many, a part of life. Richest of all our sources, though, are the stories former slaves gave of themselves. Sophia Pooley, who was then living in the Queen's Bush – some two million acres (800,000 ha) comprising parts of the present counties of Wellington, Waterloo, Dufferin, Grey, and Bruce, being made available to settlers – told her story to Benjamin Drew in 1855. He included it in a book called *The Refugee*. Like Margaret Kleine, whom we met in Chapter 1, Pooley had been a slave of Joseph Brant. Their stories, however, are quite different.

Chief Joseph Brant (Thayendanegea) was granted land in Ontario as a reward for his loyalty to the British during the American Revolution. The church he had built there – Her Majesty's Chapel of the Mohawks – is now preserved as a historic site.

I was born in Fishkill, New York State, twelve miles from
North River. My father's name was Oliver Burthen, my
mother's Dinah. I am now more than ninety years old. I was
stolen from my parents when I was seven years old, and
brought to Canada; that was long before the American
Revolution. There were hardly any white people in Canada
then – nothing here but Indians and wild beasts. . . . I was a
woman grown when the first governor of Canada came from
England; that was Governor Simcoe.

My parents were slaves in New York State. My master's
sons-in-law, came into the garden where my sister and I
were playing among the currant bushes, tied their handker-
chiefs over our mouths, carried us to a vessel, put us in the
hold, and sailed up the river. I know not how far nor how
long – it was dark there all the time. Then we came by land.
I remember when we came to Genesee – there were Indian
settlements there – Onondagas, Senecas and Oneidas. I
guess I was the first colored girl brought into Canada. The
white men sold us at Niagara to old Indian Brant, the king. I
lived with old Brant about twelve or thirteen years as nigh as
I can tell. . . .

Canada was then filling up with white people. And after
Brant went to England and kissed the queen's hand, he was
made a colonel. Then there began to be laws in Canada. . . . I
used to talk Indian better than I could English. I have forgotten some of it – there are none to talk it with now.

Brant's third wife, my mistress, was a barbarous creature.
She could talk English, but she would not. She would tell me
in Indian to do things, and then hit me with any thing that
came to hand, because I did not understand her. I have a scar
on my head from a wound she gave me with a hatchet; and
this long scar over my eye, is where she cut me with a knife.
The skin dropped over my eye; a white woman bound it up.

Brant was very angry, when he came home, at what she had done and punished her as if she had been a child. . . .

Brant had two colored men for slaves; one of them was the father of John Patten, who lives over yonder, the other called himself Simon Ganesville. There was but one other Indian that I knew who owned a slave. I had no care to get my freedom.

At twelve years old, I was sold by Brant to an Englishman in Ancaster, for one hundred dollars, – his name was Samuel Hatt, and I lived with him seven years; then the white people said I was free, and put me up to running away. He did not stop me – said he could not take the law into his own hands. Then I lived in what is now Waterloo. I married Robert Pooley, a black man. He ran away with a white woman: he is dead.

. . . I am now unable to work, and am entirely dependent on others for subsistence: but I find plenty of people in the bush to help me a good deal.

3

CRUELTY AND KINDNESS

". . . for his long and faithful services."

To the slave-traders who shipped Africans across the ocean, their captives were not humans but cargo, to be sold for maximum profit. To many plantation owners, the slaves working in their fields seemed similarly distant and impersonal; overseers (sometimes white, sometimes black) supervised the labor, and the owners themselves might have little direct contact with the workers who created their wealth.

Some owners did recognize the enormous contribution made by slaves. General Murray, the first governor of Quebec (which then also included what is now Ontario), attempted to import slaves from New York in 1763. Like many owners, he valued them for their usefulness in coping with the varied demands of pioneer life. He wrote that black slaves were the only people who could be depended upon as laborers, because the independently-minded Canadians would not work for anyone other than themselves. Another testament to the importance of their role in Canada's early development appeared in an article written in 1889:

On the faithfulness of these attendant Negroes the voyagers were in great measure dependent for their progress and their comfort. The oar, plied by their strong arm, sometimes aided the sail of their rude bateaux, and at other times replaced it; the camp often owed both safety and comfort to the skill and deftness of their not unwilling hands.

When slaves worked directly for the family – as household servants, for example – their relationships with the owners became much more complex and conflicting. Cook and mistress might fuss together over plans for a fancy dinner party; groom and master might struggle all night to save an ailing horse; children were nursed and raised and cuddled and chided by slaves. Some slaves were manumitted – given their freedom, often upon the owner's death – as thanks for their years of service. Yet this apparent sympathy could go hand in hand with casual cruelty.

Consider the inconsistent behavior of John Askin, Sr. – one of the owners of Josiah Cutten, who died on the Sandwich gallows. Years earlier, Askin had manumitted Monette, one of his female slaves. Nine years later he purchased the remaining one-half share of Jupiter and Pompey, two men he already co-owned. Soon thereafter, he agreed to dispose of a "Mualtoe [mulatta, or mixed-race] Woman" because his large family needed the room in their house, and because they needed grocery money more than they needed an extra cook.

Mixed in with the cruelty and indifference that were part of the institution of slavery are many examples of genuine fondness between owner and slave. For example, Maria Pruyn, a slave-owner from New York, married Stephen Fairfield, who was from Vermont. The couple moved to Upper Canada and owned several slaves, until the law set them free. According to one of the Fairfield descendants, the former slaves remained with the family even after they were freed. On one occasion,

Many white people found it easier and more convenient to turn a blind eye to the sermons and newspaper articles decrying slavery, and to go on living as they always had. One writer who helped change that was Harriet Beecher Stowe. Her 1852 novel Uncle Tom's Cabin *was wildly successful, and impossible to ignore.*

This passionate, dramatic novel about the evils of slavery was a bestseller, translated into twenty-three languages and sold around the world, and also reworked into a popular play. Not surprisingly, the tale was banned in the slave-owning regions of the United States. Samuel Green, a free black who was suspected of helping slaves (including his own son) escape to Canada, was sentenced to ten years in penitentiary for possessing a copy of the book.

Mott, an elderly black nurse of the family, walked a distance of 160 miles (256 km) in the cold to York to warn her former mistress that there was a plot against her property. By the time Mott arrived, her shoes had been worn right off her feet.

The family of John Baker – the slave who worked for cruel Colonel Gray – is another example of the paradox that sometimes existed. The Gray family had been slave-owners for many years, and had certainly witnessed the pain caused by the separation of families. Yet they could still show sympathy. The private thoughts of young Mr. Gray come through in a letter that he wrote in Kingston, to his cousin, on February 16, 1804, which mentions John's mother, Dorine:

> I saw some of our old friends while in the States. None was I more happy to meet than Lavine, Dorine's mother. Just as I was leaving Albany I heard from our cousin, Mrs. Garret Staats, who is living in Albany, that Lavine was living in a tavern with a man of the name of Bramley. I immediately employed a friend of mine (Mr. Ramsay, of Albany) to negotiate with the man for the purchase of her. He did so, stating that I wished to buy her freedom, in consequence of which the man readily complied with my wishes, and although he declared she was worth to him £100.00, he gave her to me for $50.00. When I saw her she was overjoyed, and appeared as happy as any person could be at the idea of seeing her child Dorine and her children once more, with whom, if Dorine wishes it, she will willingly spend the remainder of her days. I could not avoid doing this act; the opportunity seemed to have been thrown in my way by Providence, and I could not resist. She is a good servant yet, healthy and strong, and among you you may find her useful. I have promised her that she may work as much or as little as she pleases, while she lives; but from the character I have of her, idleness is not her pleasure.

Thomas John Holland knew all too well the fine line separating freedom from the abyss of slavery. In 1860, Holland escaped from Maryland, through Niagara to Canada, to join his brother William. Later, he moved to Hamilton and married Henrietta Shorts. Meanwhile, Thomas and William's parents and three sisters – still enslaved – were split up and sold off to different plantations, in revenge for the young men stealing their own freedom.

... I saw old Cato, Lavine's father, at Newark while I was at Colonel Ogden's. He is living with Mrs. Governeur, is well taken care of, and blind; poor fellow came to feel me, for he could not see. He asked affectionately after the family.

Perhaps young Mr. Gray had a gentler heart than did his father, who was so fond of beating his slaves. Or perhaps he was trying to right the wrongs done by his own family. Perhaps his actions even had an influence on the disposition of his father, for six months after this letter was written, his father wrote his last will and testament. In it, he told his executors to free his slaves, Dorine and her children, and raise a sum of money and place it in a fund so that they would not want for the necessities of life. John was given two hundred acres in Whitby Township, along with £50. His brother Simon was also given two hundred acres of land, as well as a silver watch. Whether this marked a change in character or an attack of conscience, or was simply an old man's attempt to bargain for a place in heaven, we will never know.

Because Canada did not have the huge plantations of the
southern states, more Canadian slaves worked in domestic roles,
and they tended to have a more personal relationship with their
owners. They were often referred to as servants rather than
slaves, although the softer term did nothing to change the reality
of their captivity. There may also have been more willingness to
see them as humans, with souls and a share in divine grace.
Baptisms and marriages of slaves are listed in early records of the
Catholic and Anglican churches in Canada. The Moravian missionaries who lived along the banks of the Thames River, at
Moraviantown in Upper Canada, recorded a church service in
1791 that included Indians, whites, and Negro slaves. It's difficult
now to understand how slaves and owners could kneel and pray
and vow to the same God, yet one group could presume to own
the other as surely as they owned the boots on their feet.

Although it was not uncommon for a slave to be freed upon
a master's death, it was still seen as a special reward. The majority of slaves were passed on as inheritances, along with the house
and the farm animals and the family silver. This was not done
casually, but with planning and calculation, as we see in the will
of James Girty:

In the name of God, Amen.

I, James Girty, of the Township of Gosfield, in the County
of Essex, in the Western District of Upper Canada, yeoman,
being of sound mind and memory but considering the uncertainty of human life, do make this my Last Will and in
manner following to wit:

My desire is to be buried at as little expense as decency
will permit and after the paying of all my just debts and
funeral expenses, I make the following disposition of all my
property real and personal.

To my son James Girty and to my daughter Ann or Nancy

Girty who are both now living with me, I give and devise all my lands and tenements with their appurtenances situate and being in the said Township of Gosfield ... containing two hundred acres [80 ha] or there abouts, to be divided between them ... and to their respective heirs forever.

I also bequeath to my said son James the following six Negro slaves or such of them as may be living at the time of my death, viz: Jim or James, Hannah, Joe, Jack, Betsy and Tom, and also the children which may hereafter be born of the said Hannah and Betsy. And to my daughter I bequeath my negro wench called Sall, and also a Negro woman called Nancy with her five children, which said Nancy was the property of the mother of my said children and intended by her for my said daughter and also the children who may hereafter be born of their bodies or the bodies of their children respectively.

And as to all the remaining part of the personal property which I may die possessed of, including household furniture, cattle, horses, swine, poultry, money, grain and all other descriptions of personal property, and also all the cattle and other stock which was the property of my deceased wife Betsey, an Indian woman, and the mother of my said children, and also the increase thereof, my will is that the same and every part thereof shall be equally divided between my said son and daughter share and share alike ... except the utensils of husbandry, which I give to my said son James for his own proper use and benefit, and except also my negro slave Paul, whose freedom I hereby bequeath to him for his long and faithful services.

4

TURBULENT TIMES

". . . our house was a place of refuge . . ."

For generations now, Canadians and Americans have boasted of our freedom and democracy, and the stable "undefended border" between our countries. It's not easy to cast our minds back to the mid-1700s and early 1800s – not so very long ago – when European immigrants had barely begun to settle the territory around the Great Lakes. Over fifty years the borders changed and changed again, and so did the laws about slavery.

First, in 1763, the French lost their claim to eastern North America, and the French territories (in what is now Canada) were added to the lands the British already held (in what is now the United States). There had been slaves in both French and British territories, but – for economic reasons – the greatest number of slaves had worked on the vast sugar and cotton plantations of the south.

Next, in 1775, the American states rebelled against the British Empire, and sought independence, while the territories farther north (now Canada) remained loyal to Britain. The American

George W. Hatter was a house slave in the Appalachian Mountains, in what is now West Virginia; his brother Frank was a field laborer. Their mistress favored George, and taught him to read, defying both her husband and prevailing custom. After one failed attempt, George managed to escape in 1837, at the age of nineteen. He had to leave his brother behind; Frank refused to take the risk of fleeing. After following the North Star across the states of Pennsylvania and New York, George found safety in Canada, working as a peddler in Niagara and later becoming a prosperous community leader in Buxton. It was more than forty years before the two brothers were reunited in Canada.

Revolution ended in 1783, but there was still hostility and suspicion between Britain and the United States, and the new border was far from secure. Meanwhile, families from the American states who wanted to remain British had picked up and moved north, with their households and their slaves. Those who chose to move are known as United Empire Loyalists.

In 1793, the government of Upper Canada (essentially Ontario) passed a law that decreed, among other things, that while those enslaved there would remain slaves, any slave who *entered* the territory would become free. Within ten years a similar act was passed in Lower Canada (Quebec and the Maritimes). Some of the northern U.S. states were also eliminating slavery. As word of these safe havens spread through the slave-holding states, more and more people made desperate attempts to escape to freedom. This outraged the slave-owners, who felt they were being robbed of their legal property. In 1793, the American Congress tried to resolve the problem by passing the first Fugitive Slave Act; it was now a crime for anyone to help a slave escape.

This same period – the late 1700s and early 1800s – is the time when much of Ontario began to be settled. As in most areas, early settlement followed the waterways – in this case, the lakes and rivers that make up the Great Lakes system. Among the regions first settled were the Niagara Frontier – the Niagara peninsula – and the Detroit Frontier – the area along the Detroit River between Lake Erie and Lake St. Clair. Many of the people who settled here were United Empire Loyalists.

When we think about the Underground Railroad, we generally think of routes going northward. However, there are interesting stories of the route going in reverse. Captain Matthew Elliott, a very prominent United Empire Loyalist who lived in what is now Amherstburg, Ontario, was a slave-owner around the early 1800s. The whipping post, where people were tied to be whipped, remained until the twentieth century, a vivid reminder that the respect he enjoyed from some was not universal. Elliott was a man of means, and his estate rivaled a southern plantation. An observer wrote in 1797 that Elliott

> lives as I am informed in the greatest affluence at an expense of above a thousand [pounds] a year. He possesses an extensive farm not far from the garrison stock'd with about six or seven hundred head of cattle & I am told employs fifty or sixty persons constantly about his house & farm chiefly slaves.

It is said that Elliott had brought many of his slaves from his Virginia plantation. Several of them were driven to escape his

Matthew Elliott's homestead near Amherstburg was built by his slaves in 1784. Seven years later, some of these slaves, along with Indians and whites, attended the first Protestant Moravian religious services to be held in Canada, near this spot. Elliott served as an Indian agent for the British government; the Shawnee leader Tecumseh was a friend of his, and visited here during the War of 1812.

cruel treatment. Unlike the many southern fugitives who fled north across the Detroit River, following the North Star to freedom, these refugees crossed the river to head south. Their destination was the Michigan Territory of the United States, which at the time prohibited slavery.

One of Captain Elliott's friends, Colonel Alexander McKee – also a United Empire Loyalist – had his "mollato man name Bill" escape from Upper Canada. Bill had evidently been encouraged in his flight, for McKee expressed his anger in a letter he wrote from Kingston on August 11, 1795: "a Negro man of mine whom I left in charge of my House, &c. &c. has been seduced away to General Wayne's camp." (General Anthony Wayne had fought the British successfully several times during the

American Revolution. Now that the revolution was over, he was fighting to subdue the native population.) Elliott sent a man across the border to Fort Wayne, in what is now Indiana, to recapture this fugitive. The would-be slave-catcher was rebuked by the American officers and told that the slave was now free. In a somewhat confusing argument, the officers asserted that Bill had been given his liberty because he had reached the safety of the American lines, and that he had been stolen from their country in the first place!

John Askin, Jr. – whose father's ex-slave Josiah Cutten had been hanged at Sandwich – was one of many slave-owners who wrote bitterly about such fugitives.

Askin, Matthew Elliott, and their neighbors along the Detroit frontier shared their worry about people helping escapees through an early version of the Underground Railroad that began, rather than ended, in Canada. In a letter he wrote in 1803, one of these neighbors, Alexander Grant, complained about being troubled with a "Cursed negroe wench" whom Captain Elliott had recently sold; she was now in jail, along with a black man who was also charged with theft. He went on to warn of a "great number of vagarents [vagrants] hovering about here to bring off as many negros as they can," and to say that these people were forming a town on the other side of Sandusky, Ohio. He claimed that forty black men had gone there.

In 1807, Askin, who was among those making preparations for the likely war between the United States and Canada, noted that across the river, in Detroit, "a company of Negroes" were keeping guard in fear of invasion. Interestingly, they were runaway slaves from Canada; the Americans had given them weapons to fight against their former Canadian owners.

An obituary in the October 13, 1838 edition of the newspaper *The Colored American* tells us who one of those people in Sandusky was: James Ford. (Hiram Wilson, one of the little-

The Niagara River Gorge, in 1853. The Great Lakes system was a huge barrier to fugitives, because it left them so few safe places to cross the border. Slave-hunters lurking in the border towns would pounce on anyone who might be labeled a runaway – even if that label was a lie.

known giants among anti-slavery activists in Canada – whom we shall meet later in this book – provided the information for the obituary.) Apparently, Ford was born a slave in the United States in the mid-1700s, but was able to purchase his freedom for $150 prior to "Wayne's war with the Indians." Unfortunately, during the war he was captured by ten natives in Kentucky and re-enslaved by them. They led him through the forests of Kentucky, Ohio, and Michigan, allowing him only roots and leaves to eat. They also forced him to run the gauntlet three times. (That meant running between two lines of natives while they beat him.) His captors spared his life because of the bravery he exhibited. When Ford asked them why he had been taken prisoner, as blacks did not make war on Indians, they replied that the white Americans had taken their lands; to get revenge, they stole blacks from them and sold them to the British king. Following this logic, they sold Ford to a Canadian man in Malden (now Amherstburg) for 150 pounds.

Ford was determined to regain his freedom, and persuaded two other slaves to join him. The three got into a small sailboat and set a course south across Lake Erie toward Sandusky. To keep up their strength they took along a half-bushel of biscuits, eight loaves of bread, and two pounds of sugar. Their voyage lasted from ten o'clock on Sunday night until sunrise on Tuesday morning, when they reached Cleveland, at the mouth of the Cuyahoga River. They counted themselves blessed to have sailed with favorable winds and to find friends at the end of their journey. Ford settled in Erie, Pennsylvania, for the next thirty years, and hid many other fugitive slaves in his home. He would assist American fugitives until they could get passage across the lake to Canada – the very place he himself had fled.

Near the end of his life, James Ford returned to Canada, along with his wife. The elderly couple spent their final years in St. Catharines, with their daughter Amy, who had herself married a fugitive slave. Years later, Amy Ford Martin would tell her family's story:

When we were in Erie, we lived a little way out of the village, and our house was a place of refuge for fugitives – a station of the underground railroad. Sometimes there would be thirteen or fourteen fugitives at our place. My parents used to do a great deal towards helping them on to Canada. They were sometimes pursued by their masters, and often advertised; and their masters would come right into Erie. We used to be pretty careful, and never got into any trouble on that account, that I know of. The fugitives would be told to come to our house.

5

EMANCIPATION THROUGHOUT THE EMPIRE

*". . . so many of Africa's sons here
met to-day, in a land of freedom . . ."*

U pper Canada's law of 1793, freeing newly arrived slaves, had
been spurred by the territory's first lieutenant-governor,
Colonel John Graves Simcoe, and by the sad story of Chloe Cooley.

Chloe Cooley was a slave in Queenston, but her owner determined to sell her in the United States, much against her wishes.
Witnesses heard her screams and watched in dismay as Cooley,
securely tied with ropes, was placed into a boat and carried
across the Niagara River to be delivered to a man on the other
side. There was a great outcry from the Canadians, but the owner
had the legal right to sell his slave wherever he chose.

While nothing could be done to save this unfortunate young
woman, her tragedy helped focus public attention on the evils of
slavery, and gave impetus to the campaign to establish laws to
prevent a tragedy like Chloe Cooley's from happening again.

After much debate and compromise, the act was passed on
July 9, 1793. While the slaves in Upper Canada were not freed by
this act, it provided some hope. There would be no further

John Graves Simcoe had been ardently opposed to slavery in Britain, before he was appointed Lieutenant-Governor of Upper Canada in 1792. His support was an important factor in passing the law that would eventually eliminate slavery in Canada.

introduction of slaves into the province; any children born to slaves would become free at age twenty-five; any grandchildren of those currently enslaved would be free from birth. Those who were slaves when the bill was passed would remain so until their death, unless their owners chose to free them. But eventually – step by step – slavery would be erased.

As with any compromise, there were debates and disappointments on all sides. Abolitionists had hoped to ban slavery once and for all, but many powerful families owned slaves and were strongly opposed to any law that might threaten their way of life. The only practical way to loosen the grip of slavery, when it was so prevalent, was to stop short of immediately outlawing it.

David William Smith, a member of Parliament, was one of those who were disappointed by the compromise. On June 28,

1793, he wrote from Niagara to John Askin, Sr., who then lived in the British-occupied town of Detroit:

> We have made no law to free the slaves. All those who have been brought into the Province or purchased under any authority legally exercised, are slaves to all intents and purposes and are secured as property by a certain act of Parliament. They are determined, however to have an act about slaves – part of which, I think, is well enough – part most iniquitous. I wash my hands of it. A free man who is married to a slave – his heir is declared by this act to be a slave. fye. fye. The Laws of God and Man cannot authorize it.

The dispute over slaves and slavery continued. Many blacks had come to Canada around the time of the American Revolution, as property of United Empire Loyalist families. Thomas Jefferson, one of the architects of the new United States republic, wrote a letter to the British authorities reminding them that it had been agreed, at the time of the revolution, that citizens who remained loyal to the British crown were to leave the United States quickly "without causing any destruction, or carrying away any Negroes, or other property, of the American inhabitants." Jefferson accused the British of making off with over three thousand blacks, against the protests of the Americans.

The British argued that some of the blacks had been captured during the war, and therefore rightfully belonged to the captors. Also, many had joined the British army under a promise that they would be given their freedom; the British government was opposed to going back on that promise. All in all, said the British, "every slave like every horse, which escaped or strayed from within the American lines, and came into the possession of the British army, became by the laws and rights of war, British property. . . ."

Branded by Color

The very nature of slavery in North America was based on race. For this reason, it was difficult for free blacks to distinguish themselves from slaves. In 1781, after receiving several complaints that free blacks were being seized and sold, the new governor of Canada, General Haldimand, ordered that a list be compiled of slaves belonging to Loyalists who were entering his territory. He hoped that this would show who was already a slave and who was not, and so prevent free people from being sold into slavery. It was discovered that some people had in fact been fraudulently sold by scouting parties who had brought them in from the United States. Some were sold in Montreal and some were taken to Niagara. Others were returned to previous masters.

In the early 1800s, Britain and the United States were still squabbling over who ought to own Canada, and over the matter of slavery. Slavery was still also a bitter political issue within the United States, between the northern states – who talked of morality, but in fact didn't really need slaves – and the southern states, whose wealth depended on a slave economy. And both north and south of the border there was a complicated patchwork of laws about who could be enslaved and who could not, and when, and what should happen to slaves who ran away.

In 1812, American troops crossed the Niagara River and invaded Canada. British troops fought back, supported by militias: bands of local men – farmers, craftsmen, tradesmen – with minimal military training, and whatever weapons came to hand. Blacks joined these militias along with their white neighbors, and

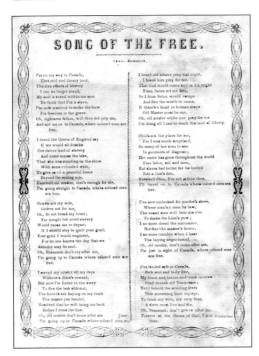

"The Song of the Free," published around 1863 and sung to the tune of "Oh Susannah," expresses the difficult choice slaves had to make: whether to stay with whatever safety they had, under the yoke of captivity, or to "strike the blow for freedom or the grave" by heading for the "cold and dreary land" of "Canada, where colored men are free." Some slave-owners deliberately spread lies about the horrors of Canada, to discourage anyone from seeking refuge there.

"I heard the Queen of England say
If we would all forsake
Our native land of slavery
And come across the lake,
That she was standing on the shore
With arms extended wide,
To give us all a peaceful home
Beyond the rolling tide...."

Although Queen Victoria didn't offer the personal welcome promised by "The Song of the Free," she personified the freedom found within her vast empire, and her subjects came in all colors.

The Battle of Queenston Heights, near Niagara, during the War of 1812.
In the foreground lies the dying Sir Isaac Brock, military commander and
administrator of Upper Canada, cut down by an American sharpshooter.
Note the native warriors on the right; Captain Runchey's Company of
Coloured Men also fought in this battle.

When he came from England, Brock brought with him his African cook,
Amy Malawice. She remained in Amherstburg after his death, and many
of her descendants still live in south-western Ontario.

participated in many of the battles. For them, the threat of
American domination held a special terror: if America con-
quered Canada, they might be driven into slavery once again.

    Former members of Butler's Rangers (a Loyalist regiment
during the American Revolution) who had settled in Essex and
Kent counties were part of the Kent Militia. Richard Pierpont,
an ex-slave who had been kidnapped as a child from Africa and
who had previously fought during the American Revolution,
petitioned the government to allow the formation of a "colored"

company. (A company is usually about one hundred soldiers; a regiment might have five hundred to a thousand.) His request was granted, and Pierpont, then in his sixties, was among the soldiers who served in "Captain Runchey's Company of Coloured Men." Although the ranks of such regiments were filled with blacks, white officers were in command. Officials had a certain faith in the abilities of blacks as soldiers, but no confidence in their ability to lead.

The Americans had expected an easy victory. They were to be disappointed; after two years of fighting the war ended without benefit to either side, and both returned to their original 1812 borders. (The success of the British resistance was due, in part, to support from the native Shawnee people and their leader Tecumseh, who had been defeated in their homeland by the Americans.)

The War of 1812 added fire to the issue of slavery and fugitives. In 1826 the Secretary of State for the United States suggested to his British counterparts that they reach an agreement whereby slaves from one country who escaped to the other would be returned; this request continued to resurface over many years. The British continued to insist that their laws gave freedom to any slave who found a haven on their soil, including Canada.

However, this did not mean that blacks were welcome. In 1832, Benjamin Lundy, one of the leading abolitionists in the United States, visited Canada to observe what life was like for blacks. While visiting Brantford, he noted that they could escape from America but not from mistreatment:

The white emigrants from the United States retain all the prejudices here that they formerly held against the colored people in their native country. And the latter, being admitted

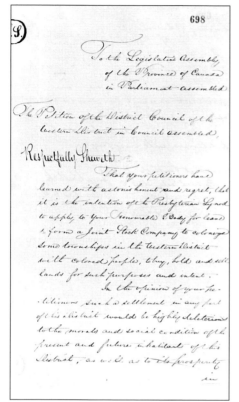

This petition, sent to the government of Upper Canada in 1849, expressed "astonishment and regret" that the Presbyterian Church was planning to support the Elgin Settlement, a colony for ex-slaves. Such a settlement, the writer predicted, would be "highly deleterious to the morals and social conditions" of other residents.

to equal privileges with them under this government are accused of being "saucy."

Mary O'Brien and her husband were among the white settlers who were notable for their support of blacks. The O'Briens moved first to Vaughan Township, north of Toronto, in 1828, and later to Shanty Bay, in Oro Township, on Lake Simcoe. There had been a growing black community in Oro since 1819. Some of those "men of color" who defended their country during the War of 1812 had been given grants of land in Oro, not only as a reward for their support, but also to provide a line of warning and defense against any invasion that might be threatened from Michigan, across Lake Huron and Georgian Bay.

LOCATION TICKET.
(NOT TRANSFERABLE)

PURSUANT to a General Order in Council of the 19th January 1820, respecting Militia Grants, and under the Certificate No. ____ of the Adjutant General of Militia, in favor of ____ in the County of ____ of the Township of ____ in the ____ District of ____ as a ____ in Captain's ____ Corps of Colour

I do hereby assign to the said ____

____ in the Township of ____ in the County of ____ in the ____ District ____ containing ____ Acres, subject to the Settling duties required by an Order in Council of the 20th October 1818: that is to say,—to clear and fence Five Acres for every Hundred Acres granted; to erect a Dwelling House of 16 feet by 20; and to clear one half of the Road in front of each Lot. The whole to be performed within Two Years from the date of this Ticket.

N. B.—On the 21st of February 1820, His Excellency the Lieutenant Governor was pleased to direct that the clearing of half the Road, and cutting down without clearing, one Chain in depth, from the Road, along the front of each Lot—be considered as part of the Five acres per Hundred required.

Given at the Surveyor General's Office, at York, U. C, this ____ day of ____ 182_

No. of Certificate S. G. O.

____

This "location ticket," dated 1820, assigns a hundred acres (40 ha) of Ontario farmland to "Robert Jupiter, A Man of Colour," in recognition of his military service in "Captain Runchey's Corps of Colour." Now all Jupiter had to do was clear and fence five acres, clear half the road area, and build a good-sized house – within the next two years.

The O'Briens were both friends and employers of blacks. Mary O'Brien spoke of a large tract of land north of the lake that had been acquired by blacks, and dismissed the attitudes of others in her neighborhood:

> I am provoked to see that some of our wise members have resolved that the Negro settlement is likely to disturb the peace of the neighbourhood, but I hope no notice has been, or is like to be, taken of such nonsense.

Although prejudice was certainly very strong, however, the fact remained that – in the words of John Moore of London – "The law here is stronger than the mob."

Black regiments — sometimes referred to as "The Black Defenders" – continued to serve the country. At times their role was military. In 1837 there were local rebellions in both Upper Canada and Lower Canada, and many people feared that the

This modest structure, the African Methodist Episcopal Church of Oro, was built in Edgar, in 1849, by the blacks who settled in Oro County – the potential "peace-disturbers" feared by some white residents. The black settlers eventually moved away, discouraged by Oro's poor soil and severe weather. Only the church, now a National Historic Site, remains.

United States would take advantage of the unrest to mount another invasion. The Lieutenant-Governor of Upper Canada proudly proclaimed before Parliament that "the coloured population" had come to Niagara by the wagonload and volunteered to fight to keep the Americans out of their new country.

At other times the black regiments worked in a peaceful capacity. One of their assignments was to build a road between Cayuga and Canboro, in the Niagara Peninsula. They built their homes along this road, and were settled in by 1841.

Slavery was finally, officially abolished throughout the British Empire, including Canada, by an Emancipation Act that took effect on August 1, 1834. South of the border, though, many states still allowed slavery. It was already a crime to help a slave escape, as decreed by the first Fugitive Slave Act; after 1850, under the second Fugitive Slave Act, all "good citizens" of the United States were legally obliged to cooperate in catching such runaways.

Jarmain Wesley Loguen, a fugitive slave and anti-slavery activist, worked as a minister and a newspaper publisher. In his spare time, with the help of his wife and daughter, he ran two stations on the Underground Railroad – one in his home, another in his church. He wrote passionately of the black community's determination to keep slavery out of Canada – "these able-bodied and daring refugees are the most reliable fortress of national strength on the Canadian frontiers" – and predicted that, if slavery began threatening the free blacks of the northern states, "the blacks of Canada will be found overleaping national boundaries; and, gathering the sympathizing forces in the line of march, will imprint upon the soil of slavery as bloody a lesson as was ever written."

Fugitives who reached the northern states might be able to live freely, but they were always at risk of being recaptured, and sent back into misery. The only true safety lay in Canada.

But Canada was a long way away. Anyone headed there needed directions, and food and money, and safe places to hide along the way. And while people along the route might want to help – while they might truly believe that slavery was evil and oppressive – if they followed their consciences, if they helped a fugitive or even failed to report one, they risked paying a heavy price. They might be fined or jailed. They might even be beaten or murdered, by irate slave-owners.

Thus began the legendary Underground Railroad, the secret network of good-hearted people, black and white, who risked their safety and their lives to help fugitives find their way to Canada. Over thirty thousand people are estimated to have found safety and a new home in Canada prior to the American Civil War, and the constitutional amendment of 1865, which finally put an end to slavery in the United States.

Not all Canadians welcomed the refugees – there was opposition to their arrival, and a great deal of prejudice – but black settlements sprang up across Ontario. In Canada, at least these people who had been so long oppressed were optimistic that the laws of the land would ensure their freedom. Each year, August 1 – the anniversary of the emancipation of all slaves in the British Empire – would be a day of celebration. It would also be a day to reflect on the many others – including family and friends – who still had no cause to celebrate. On August 1, 1839, the people of Toronto would gather to remember:

> We are here met to celebrate the anniversary of our
> Emancipation from Slavery, and, although there may be many
> of us who have never been so unfortunate as to have been
> subjected to the yoke of Slavery, we cannot but feel all alike

Austin Steward gave up his successful butcher and grocery shop in New York State to move to Canada. In 1831 he became organizer and director of the black settlement of Wilberforce. His understanding of business was a valuable asset to the residents, many of whom had no commercial experience. Steward eventually became a full-time minister.

grateful to the British Monarch, and to the British people, for the Emancipation of each of our race, as were subjected to that inhuman yoke. It must be more than gratifying to all of you, as it certainly is to me, to see so many of Africa's sons here met to-day, in a land of freedom, in a land where we enjoy the principles of freemen. How grateful then should we all be, to the people, for the measure of liberty and freedom, which they have extended to us; and how can we help contrasting their liberality, with the cruel selfishness of the self-called freemen in the adjoining Republic, where there are millions of their fellow men held in bondage . . .?

6

SETTING OUT FOR THE UNKNOWN

"... they always had to pilot their own canoe ..."

The American forays into Canada during the War of 1812 had one curious and unexpected consequence. Among the soldiers who crossed the border into Ontario were a good number of slave-owners, many of whom had told their slaves horror stories about the icy, deadly wasteland of Canada. When the slave-owners returned home to America after the war, they naturally spoke to their friends and families more honestly about the foreign country they had ventured into. Often their conversations were overheard by their slaves, who passed this priceless information around the slave community in whispers of secrecy and wonder.

Canada was *not* just a cold and barren wasteland! Blacks lived there, raised their families, and prospered in a country whose laws made no distinction by color! They even bore arms and fought for their country – because they were free, because they, of all people, knew the value of freedom!

These rumors of liberty conjured up many images in their minds. According to twelve-year-old Thomas Johnson,

> Freedom was frequently before my mind. I heard that the Queen of England had given large sums of money to set the coloured people free, and if I could get to Canada I would be safe. And here let me mention, that we had the idea on the plantation that the Queen was black. Accustomed to nothing but cruelty at the hands of the white people, we had never imagined that a great ruler, so kind to coloured people, could be otherwise than black. To me she was the subject of many a dream: she often came before my mind, laid hold upon me, and compelled me to imagine what kind of a person she was. I used to picture her as a black lady, amidst numerous coloured attendants, surrounded by a grandeur that exceeded all I had ever seen amongst the wealthy white people. And then I thought what a happy thing it must be to live under the reign of so good a Queen.

The slaves' masters were also very much aware of the allure Canada had for their "property," and took steps to diminish it. One slave, J. Lindsey, was told that in Canada people had to pay half their wages to the queen every day – and that it was so cold they had to break the ice with their farm implements before they could cut the grass. Another, Harrison Webb, from Henry County, Kentucky, had been warned that the Detroit River, which separates the United States from Canada, was a thousand miles wide. To further discourage him from running away, Webb's master had told him that if any of his slaves should try to escape "I would follow him to hell, and if I saw him in there I would just jump in and get him." Even a man living on the American side of the Niagara River, far from the slave-owning states, tried to

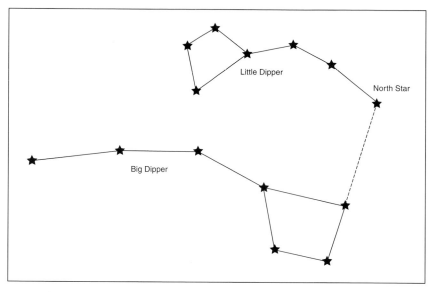

Many fugitives had no map or compass to guide them. They traveled mostly at night, under cover of darkness. On clear nights they relied on the stars to lead them to Canada; the constellations of the Big Dipper and Little Dipper are easy to spot, and point to the beacon of the North Star. On cloudy nights it was all too easy to get turned around and to travel the wrong way.

dissuade a frightened group of refugees from making that short trip to freedom. He claimed that he had just returned from Canada, where he had seen six blacks lying beside the road with their heads cut off, and others hanging from trees with the crows eating their eyes out.

Warnings of terrors like these dissuaded some would-be runaways, but others were determined to take whatever risk was necessary. Nor were they frightened off by the prospect of being stopped by slave patrols, captured by bounty hunters, or chained, whipped, sold, or even killed by vengeful owners. Many of them were convinced that, no matter what awaited them if they fled, it could not be worse than a life of slavery. Still, these dire warnings were a reminder that escape would call for great caution, and greater daring.

There are many romanticized tales of the Underground
Railroad that focus on the network of rescuers, with their secret
codes and signals, their camouflaged hiding-places, their quick-
witted excuses and diversions. Often overshadowed are the actual
experiences of the fugitives themselves, and their courage and
stamina. Most attempts at flight were solitary undertakings, or
were carried out by a small company of friends or family
members. Far from being passive recipients of the good deeds of
others, thousands achieved their freedom unaided.

Many runaways had heard rumors of abolitionists – people
who believed that slavery was an evil that ought to be ended,
people who might even help fugitives along their way – but it
was impossible to be absolutely sure who was a friend and who
was not. Trusting the wrong person could lead to punishment
and misery, and perhaps death. William Wells Brown wrote that
when he escaped in 1834, he had no knowledge of the
Underground Railroad. In any case, he was afraid to trust
anyone, no matter what color. He recalled that the North Star
that guided him was usually his only friend. Even a group of abolitionists of the time who deserved great credit for their own
anti-slavery activities felt more inclined to give praise than to
receive it; they resolved "That from the renowned Frederick
Douglass down to the obscurest fugitive slave, there is not one
who deserves not our praise for the skill with which he contrived
his escape, and the courage with which he accomplished it."

Examples are plentiful. Twenty-three-year-old Alfred Jones
of London learned that he was to be sold, but he had acquired
enough familiarity with letters that he was able to write a pass
for himself. A pass was the written permission that an owner
gave a slave to allow the slave to travel unsupervised; this pass
had to be presented when requested, to confirm that the slave
really was traveling with permission. Although Jones' pass was
poorly spelled and awkwardly written, it fooled those who

Frederick Douglass was indeed renowned. Born a slave, he never knew his father. His mother died when he was a child, and he endured cruel beatings and starvation. When he was twenty-one he disguised himself and escaped to the north, became a famous abolitionist, wrote a book about his experiences, edited several newspapers, including the North Star, Frederick Douglass' Paper, *and* Douglass' Monthly, *and took part in the Underground Railroad. In 1889 this one-time slave became the U.S. minister to the island of Haiti.*

Anti-slavery leaders met at St. Lawrence Hall, in downtown Toronto, for their 1851 North American Convention. Frederick Douglass made two stirring speeches against slavery in this building, which still stands today.

checked it, because no one thought a slave would be able to read or write.

John Francis sailed with his father in an open boat for over ten days, without water and with little food. They finally reached the safety of the Queen's Bush. Francis, whose mother had been sold away when he was a child, quipped that he had been sold three times: "first, for debt; then I was traded off; the third time I sold myself to myself."

Naturally, southern slave-holders did their best to convince their slaves that so-called abolitionists were up to one trick or another, and could never be trusted. Robert Nelson ran away from Kentucky before he could be sold to a Louisiana cotton farm. Although he had heard about the abolitionists, he was afraid to confide in any white person. He had been assured that some people were willing to buy him to give him his freedom, but he had also heard rumors that they would in fact just sell him again. Not until he was safely in the large black community of Colchester Township, in Essex County, could he bring himself to believe that the promises of the abolitionists were true.

Runaways had to survive using whatever means were available to them. Some managed to take a little food when they left; others gathered what they could along the way. Indian corn, potatoes, and other edibles could be taken from fields and gardens if they were in season. Edward Hicks escaped as he was being transported from Virginia to New Orleans, and survived for part of the journey on sassafras leaves and water. Another fugitive told of being so thirsty that he would drink water out of the imprints made in the mud by horses' hoofs. Along the way, barns, haystacks, ditches, hollow logs, or caves might occasionally offer a bit of shelter and concealment.

On June 4, 1851, *The Voice of the Fugitive* – a newspaper published in Sandwich, Ontario – carried a story of a slave who used the rumor of untrustworthy abolitionists to his benefit. John

After being sold and separated from her family, fifteen-year-old Anna Marie Weems resolved to escape from the cruel couple who owned her. She arranged to meet an Underground Railroad conductor in front of the White House, in Washington, D.C. By dressing as a boy and pretending to be the conductor's coachman, she managed to elude slave-catchers seeking the $500 reward for her capture, and eventually reached the safety of her uncle's home in Dresden, Ontario.

Moore was a slave in Kentucky who had (as sometimes happened, though certainly not always) taken the surname of his master, Elijah Moore. John first escaped and lived in the free state of Indiana for two months, saving the money he earned there. Then he returned to his owner and gave him his money, saying that

The Voice of the Fugitive *was published by Henry Bibb, a passionate abolitionist who had escaped slavery in Kentucky. In addition to arguing against racism, Bibb's paper offered practical help to ex-slaves who arrived in Canada, looking for work and struggling to settle into their new home.*

freedom was not what he had expected it to be, and that the abolitionists were not to be relied upon. Elijah was so taken by John's "honesty" that he welcomed him back, despite warnings from neighbors that the escapee had only returned so he could rescue his family, who were enslaved on a plantation nearby.

The master of John's wife was especially suspicious, and refused to let John visit his plantation. John pretended to have no further interest in his wife, but he secretly visited her after midnight. The slaves hid their affection for each other so well that the wife's owner finally agreed to let John come and take away any belongings he might have in his wife's cabin. To further prove that the relationship was over, John used the opportunity to abuse "his wife like a dog so far as words would go, and said that he never wanted her to speak to him again." The wife's owner was so convinced by what he had witnessed that he loosened his rules and began to allow John's wife to leave his property occasionally. Mrs. Moore seized both the opportunity and her bold husband, and took an extended leave – all the way to Canada.

The Chief Justice Robinson, *with its steam-driven paddle wheel, carried many fugitives to freedom. Paddle-wheelers remained a major form of transport in Canada, for both cargo and passengers, throughout the 1800s.*

Fear and mistrust might accompany fugitives the entire distance to their final destination. Circumstances led some people to relent and ask for help – but others soldiered on alone, no matter how desperate their situation.

The Niagara River was a major, final crossing point that separated success from failure. An article in the *Niagara Mail* newspaper, in 1853, tells the story of Ben Hockley, who was almost at the end of his journey, having come all the way from Tennessee. Now he had this one more obstacle to overcome. He was afraid to try to get passage to the Canadian side on one of the steamships, so he used a gate as a raft. However, the current was so strong that he was swept along for about twenty miles (32 km) and was floating out toward Lake Ontario. Fortunately the crew of the steamer *Chief Justice Robinson* saw him, and they were able to pull him aboard ship, to complete his crossing to freedom.

The journey was always long and difficult. At times, there was assistance. Much of the time, there was not. W. H. Lyford, an

This extraordinary photo shows fugitives crossing the Rappahannock River, in the slave-owning state of Virginia, on their way north. The picture was taken in 1862, during the American Civil War, and in the early days of photography.

abolitionist from Illinois, provided a fitting tribute to this man clinging to his gate, and to all those other brave and desperate travelers: "I do not know of any fugitives ever being transported by anyone, they always had to pilot their own canoe, with the little help that they received."

7

THE KINDNESS OF STRANGERS

". . . to do what I could for the emancipation
of my brethren yet in chains . . ."

Despite the fear of betrayal that haunted so many refugee slaves, often, in order to survive, they had no choice but to trust their lives to the hands of strangers. Walking seemingly endless miles through unknown territories left them in a state of physical and emotional exhaustion. Fear, uncertainty, and hunger rattled the resolve of even the most determined freedom-seeker. Harsh laws and punishments were directed at runaways, and the most casual encounter might lead to arrest, and the horrors that followed. Worst of all were the professional slave-hunters, who lived off the rewards they collected by spotting or tracking down refugees before they reached safety.

The answer was the network of resolute people and temporary havens that became known as the Underground Railroad. Because it was illegal to help escaping slaves – and because the penalties could be severe – details of the network were secrets to be revealed only to those who could be trusted. Their communications often used railroad terms. Safe houses, where people could hide and rest

STOCKHOLDERS

OF THE UNDERGROUND

R. R. COMPANY

Hold on to Your Stock!!

The market has an upward tendency.
By the express train which arrived this morning at 3 o'clock, fifteen thousand dollars worth of human merchandise, consisting of twenty-nine able bodied men and women, fresh and sound, from the Carolina and Kentucky plantations, have arrived safe at the depot on the other side, where all our sympathising colonization friends may have an opportunity of expressing their sympathy by bringing forward donations of ploughs, farming utensils, pick axes and hoes, and not old clothes; as these emigrants all can till the soil. N.B.– Stockholders don't forget, the meeting to-day at 2 o'clock at the ferry on the Canada side. All persons desiring to take stock in this prosperous company, be sure to be on hand.

Detroit, April 19, 1853. **By Order of the BOARD OF DIRECTORS.**

Abolitionists enjoyed using railway terms even when secrecy was not an issue – as in this exuberant notice of safely transported fugitives in need of useful tools "and not old clothes."

and receive food, clothing, and directions, were called stations, and were run by station-masters. Those who guided fugitives along the way were known as agents or conductors. Messages sometimes described refugees as passengers or cargo.

Although we will never know how many thousands of escape attempts were unsuccessful, it was not uncommon for someone to run away several times before finally escaping. Many never succeeded. With the Underground Railroad, however, the chance of reaching the north and freedom became significantly better.

Betsey Robinson, of Fort Erie, described details of her memories of the early Underground Railroad. Upon the death of their owner, Betsey's family, which included her parents and seven children, feared being sent from their Virginia plantation to the New Orleans slave market. For a week Betsey's mother hid food away, while her father acquired three letters from white anti-slavery sympathizers in the south. The family would use these letters to introduce themselves to strangers who would aid them along their way. The family traveled for weeks, sometimes hiding in the mountains, which Betsey said were full of rattlesnakes, wolves, and deer. Upon reaching Pennsylvania, they found Quakers who helped them. They later found many others who also had a generous spirit, and assisted them in various ways until they reached their final destination, across the Niagara River. Even with help, the family's ordeal was dreadful; they walked the entire distance from Virginia to Ontario.

Friends and Quakers

The people we call Quakers are members of the Religious Society of Friends, formed in England in the 1600s. The state of Pennsylvania was originally granted to a Quaker, William Penn, and many Quakers settled there; the name of the capital, Philadelphia, means "brotherly love." In 1786, in a very early reference to a budding "underground railroad," George Washington refers to a Society of Quakers in Philadelphia that had formed to help slaves escape. Quakers have traditionally worked for social justice, and many were involved in the abolitionist cause.

Another successful escapee, Henry Morehead, recalled his family's trip and suffering from the safety of his new home in London:

I left slavery a little more than a year ago. I brought my wife and three children with me, and had not enough to bring us through. My owners did not know that we were coming. I left

John Anderson's life was especially perilous. He fled Missouri in 1853, avoiding recapture by stabbing and killing his assailant. Reaching Canada, he settled first in Windsor and then in Caledonia (south of present-day Hamilton). Seven years later, though, he quarreled with another ex-slave, who went to Canadian authorities with the news that Anderson was wanted for murder. Anderson was arrested but judges couldn't agree on whether he should be sent back to the United States. British abolitionists took the case before the Queen's Court in England, and Anderson was eventually released on a technicality.

because they were about selling my wife and children to the South. I would rather have followed them to the grave, than to the Ohio River to see them go down. I knew it was death or victory – so I took them and started for Canada. I was pursued, – my owners watched for me in a free State, but to their sad disappointment, I took another road. A hundred miles further on, I saw my advertisements again offering $500 for me and my family. I concluded that as money would do almost any thing, I ought to take better care, – and I took the underground railroad. I was longer on the road than I should have been without my burden; one child was nine months old, one two years old, and one four. The weather was cold, and my feet were frostbitten, as I gave my wife my socks to pull on over her shoes. With all the sufferings of the frost and the fatigues of travel, it was not so bad as the effects of slavery.

Pleas at the Court House in Cincinnati, in the County of Hamilton, and State of Ohio, of the Hamilton County Probate Court, within and for said County, at a session thereof held at the place aforesaid on the Thirteenth day of October in the year of our Lord one Thousand eight hundred and fifty eight before the Honorable George H, Hilton sole Judge of said Court,

The State of Ohio } s.s.
Hamilton County } **Be it Remembered**
That at a session of the probate Court within and for said County, held at the Court House in Cincinnati, on the Thirteenth day of October in the year of our Lord, one Thousand eight hundred and fifty eight before The Honorable George H, Hilton sole Judge of said Court, the following amongst other procedings were then and there had, to wit,

Personally appeared in open Court Mary Kirk and brought with her into open Court Susan Holton, and John M, Scott Holton and Laura Dorcas Holton Children of the said Susan, and the said Mary Kirk stated in open Court, That she brought said persons from the state of Kentucky into the state of Ohio for the purpose of Emancipating them, and the Court now find and adjudge that the said Susan Holton and Jane M, Scott Holton and Laura

Laura Dorcas Holton was free before she crossed the border into Canada. In 1858 a five-page handwritten court document recorded that a widow named Mary Kirk had brought her slaves, Susan Holton and her children – three-year-old John and fifteen-month-old Laura Dorcas – "from the state of Kentucky to the state of Ohio for the purposes of Emancipating them." The mother paid Mary Kirk one dollar for her family's freedom, a token to make the transaction legal. Although the court document recognized her freedom, perhaps Susan didn't trust this guarantee; she promptly moved her family to Ontario.

The Underground Railroad would change and evolve over time, but it remained essential to the cause of freedom even in the final days of slavery.

Harrison Webb – the man who had been warned that the Detroit River was a thousand miles wide – became a passenger in the 1860s. By this time eleven of the slave-owning states (the Confederacy) were at war with the other states (the Union). Webb's master joined the Confederate Army, and Webb seized the chance to make his escape. He had almost reached the Ohio River before he learned of the Underground Railroad. Reverend Mason, of Madison, Indiana, provided a man to guide Webb and two others; this was Webb's first introduction to an Underground Railroad agent, or conductor. Traveling only at night, the runaways survived by eating turnips and potatoes and anything else they could find. A hollow tree was a daytime hiding-place where they might uneasily grab a little bit of sleep. At one point they were forced to hide in a cave for over a week, when pursuers got too close. It seemed to them that the free state of Indiana had even more slave-catchers than the slave state of Kentucky.

Once they reached Indianapolis, their way became easier. Webb and several other runaways were loaded into a covered wagon, covered with bedclothes, and driven to "a big town with a big river." Webb recalled that this trip had taken about a week. Upon reaching the river's edge, the human cargo on the wagon were told to get into a boat, and they were paddled over to the other side of the river. After reaching Ontario, Webb would be preoccupied with finding a new home – which he did, in Hamilton and later in Buxton. But he recalled that his very first thought on reaching Canada was a wish that he could see his master's face once more, just so he could laugh at him.

Although the way was difficult for Harrison Webb, Betsey Robinson, and Henry Morehead, and their families, their ordeal pales in comparison to what many others suffered. The very title of one book – *The Narrative of the Life of J.D. Green, A Runaway Slave from Kentucky. Containing an Account of His Three Escapes, In 1839, 1846 and 1848* – tells us that Green was one of those people whose luck is not always the best.

In his first attempt, Green stowed away on a ship bound for New York by hiding under bales of cotton. In New York he befriended a black man who took him to a station of the Underground Railroad, from which the conductors planned to send him to Toronto. Unfortunately, before the plan could be completed, Green was found by his master, taken to prison, placed in chains, and ordered by a magistrate to be returned to slavery.

At one point on his return trip south, Green's shackles were removed, as they were contrary to the laws of the state of Ohio. Further along the route, other blacks made an unsuccessful attempt at rescue, wounding several officers in the process. Green was then locked away in a ship's cabin. Soon the ship's captain entered and asked the slave if he could swim. When told that he could, the captain said he would stop the paddle wheels that drove the ship long enough for Green to jump out the window, into Lake Erie, so that he could swim to shore. When the captain saw that Green was clear of the paddle wheels, he ordered the engine to be started again. As for Green, he swam to the Cleveland lighthouse, where he was cared for by a group of both blacks and whites. His freedom was short-lived, however, as his luck again ran out before he could reach Canada. A man who had purchased him from his original owner, speculating that Green could be caught before he reached Canada, captured him. This time he was returned to slavery in Kentucky, on board the steamer *Pike, No. 3*.

A year later, Green decided to attempt another escape. As it happens, he stowed away on *Pike, No. 3*, the same ship that had returned him to slavery. Conductors in Cincinnati dressed him in women's clothes and sent him to Cleveland, where he boarded

Oliver Parnell, a fugitive who settled in Canada and eventually donated land for the British Methodist Episcopal Church in Niagara Falls. The white child with him is Margaret Cadham, who later described him as "a soft spoken, wonderfully kind man" who escaped slavery with help from the Underground Railroad, swam across the "Upper River pushing a small trunk," and henceforth refused ever to step across the bridge into the United States: "you could never convince him he would not go back to Slavery."

a steamboat that carried him to Buffalo. After taking the train for Niagara Falls, he boarded the *Chief Justice Robinson* – the ship that rescued that solitary man floating on a gate – and made his final escape to Toronto.

The Great Lakes, and the rivers connecting them, formed a double obstacle blocking the path to Canada. The crossing itself could be dangerous, of course, whether it traversed choppy rivers, broad lakes, or treacherous ice. As well, since there were so few ways to get across, slave-catchers knew where to lie in wait. They haunted border crossings and shipping piers, waiting for their prey. Fortunately, agents of the Underground Railroad knew that their help would often be needed in these places.

The November 5, 1852 issue of *Frederick Douglass' Paper* carries an interesting article about one of the clashes between predators and rescuers, in Rochester, New York. The story relates that two black women and several children were dragged off a boat by the city marshal, who was acting under the direction of a man from Kentucky who claimed to be their owner. The blacks were taken before the mayor, but a group of both blacks and whites crowded his office and made a rush for the door, hustling the runaways out. By this time they had missed the evening steamboats, so they were forced to take a sailboat to Ontario. The slave-hunters tried to get a sailboat to chase them, but no one in the city would agree to help.

There is an even more touching aspect to this story. One of the young women seized was holding her baby in her arms. She jerked herself away from the slave-catcher, ran a little way off, placed her baby on the ground, and then went back to the slave-catcher. After she was led to the mayor's office, someone brought her baby to her. Believing that she would be returned to slavery, the poor mother denied that the child was hers – hoping that someone would take her dear child and raise the child in freedom.

Although William Wells Brown had no knowledge of the Underground Railroad when he made his escape (see Chapter 6), he later became intimately familiar with it. Indeed, he would be one of the best-known anti-slavery activists, as a lecturer, writer, and conductor. Brown had been born into slavery in Lexington, Kentucky, around 1814 – he was the son of a white man but his mother was a slave, and so was he. He spent most of his early life in and around St. Louis, Missouri, where he worked at many jobs: as a house servant, in the fields, in a tavern, in a printing shop, and in a medical office. His last master was a slave-trader who took William on three trips down the Mississippi, between the St. Louis and New Orleans slave markets. When he was approaching the age of twenty, he decided to make his break for freedom.

Brown's journey, like that of many others, was a more solitary escape than we commonly think of when we associate fugitive slaves with the Underground Railroad. But although he did not pass from station to station, guided by various conductors, he was not without help.

Brown's autobiography describes his escape as well as the fascinating details of those early years. Entitled *Narrative of William W. Brown, A Fugitive Slave. Written by Himself*, it was wildly successful and sold many copies in North America and Britain. His words of dedication in the beginning of the book show how gratefully he recalled the help he had received from a stranger:

> THIRTEEN years ago, I came to your door, a weary fugitive from chains and stripes. I was a stranger, and you took me in. I was hungry, and you fed me. Naked was I, and you clothed me. Even a name by which to be known among men, slavery had denied me. You bestowed upon me your own. Base, indeed, should I be, if I ever forget what I owe to you, or do anything to disgrace that honored name!

As a slight testimony of my gratitude to my earliest benefactor, I take the liberty to inscribe to you this little narrative of the sufferings from which I was fleeing when you had compassion upon me. In the multitude that you have succored, it is very possible that you may not remember me; but until I forget God and myself, I can never forget you.

Your grateful friend,
WILLIAM WELLS BROWN.

This fervent dedication is "TO WELLS BROWN, OF OHIO," whom we today would call a conductor. When this Quaker gentleman had taken in the fleeing slave named William – just William, with no surname – he had told him that a free man should have more than just a first name, and he had given him the addition of his own full name. Acts of personal kindness such as this were the heart and the foundation of the Underground Railroad.

The newly named William Wells Brown had hoped to get passage on a boat to Ontario, but Lake Erie was partially frozen over, so the ships were not running. He was forced to wait until the waterways were open again. When spring came, instead of catching a boat to Canada, he took a job working as a free man on a steamship. In his new job, Brown was able to aid others as he himself had been aided. He records that while he was working on the boats he would always arrange for fugitive slaves to be carried across to Canada. Sometimes he managed to hide four or five at one time, and he could count sixty-nine being transported in one single year. He took special pride in later finding seventeen of them all living in the small village of Malden (Amherstburg). In a short time he had gone from knowing nothing of the anti-slavery movement, to being an important part of it.

*Lewis Jackson lived only sixty-two years, but in that time his world
changed dramatically. When he was born in 1825, slavery was legal
throughout America and the British Empire, and there was nowhere to
hide. By the time he died, soon after losing his wife, Mary, slavery had
been abolished in all these territories. When did the pair come to Ontario?
Did they have a good life there? Did they leave a family of free children
and grandchildren? This tombstone they share, in a wooded lot, raises so
many questions.*

Brown's narrative also records how he, like many others, was
inspired to become part of the Underground Railroad:

I purchased some books, and at leisure moments perused
them with considerable advantage to myself. While at
Cleveland, I saw, for the first time, an anti-slavery newspaper.

It was the *"Genius of Universal Emancipation,"* published by Benjamin Lundy; and though I had no home, I subscribed for the paper. It was my great desire, being out of slavery myself, to do what I could for the emancipation of my brethren yet in chains, and while on Lake Erie, I found many opportunities of "helping their cause along."

8

SOME NAMES NOT FORGOTTEN

"I have wrought in the day – you in the night."

Secrecy was the best protection for the men and women who worked on the Underground Railroad. Routes and stations were carefully disguised, and changed if necessary. Many neighbors, and even some relatives, had no idea who among them was living a dangerous life as a station-master or conductor. Fugitives who reached freedom were careful not to reveal the identities of those who had helped them.

The silence was vital, but it had one sad result: the names of many of these heroes and heroines have been lost to history.

Some of them are known to us, though, and are justly celebrated. Among the most famous are a Quaker couple, Levi and Catherine Coffin, whose home was an important station in the Underground Railroad.

The Coffins raised money to send slaves to places like Detroit, Sandusky, and other border crossing points. Thanks in part to his book *Reminiscences of Levi Coffin*, their work in Indiana and Ohio is firmly entrenched in history. This

Catherine and Levi Coffin. Because their home was on the intersection of three different escape routes, and sheltered many fugitives, it has been called the Grand Central Station of the Underground Railroad. Note that Mrs. Coffin is dressed very plainly; Quakers disapproved of personal vanity.

autobiography relates many fascinating stories of Coffin and those he was involved with – like George de Baptiste, who became one of the leading agents in Detroit, helping refugees cross the river into Ontario.

Coffin himself made several trips to Ontario, to meet some of the people he had helped escape. He traveled to many black settlements and he was always pleased to reminisce about daring escapes, and to see the progress the former slaves were making. While staying in one of the buildings at the Amherstburg mission, with the missionary Isaac Rice, he noted that some of the families had such good farms that they were now more successful than their former masters.

One fascinating story that Levi Coffin and several others told is also a frustrating one, for it straddles that hazy line between fact and fiction.

Some of the people who reached Canada through the Coffins' help. Levi Coffin also raised money to help the fugitives build new lives.

The love between mother and child is perhaps the strongest human tie. There was no greater incentive for a woman to escape than the fear of being separated from her child. The drama of this threat is one reason why Harriet Beecher Stowe's book, *Uncle Tom's Cabin*, was so wildly successful; it tells the story of Eliza Harris, a young woman who learns that her child is to be sold away from her. Eliza runs to the thawing Ohio River, the southern border of the non-slave state of Ohio, with her baby in arms, and jumps from ice floe to ice floe to escape her master, who is in close pursuit. Another man watches in disbelief from the Ohio shore and helps Eliza reach sympathetic friends, who eventually assist mother and child to Canada. No wonder the story captured the imagination and sympathy of people around the world.

Some accounts say that Eliza's heart-rending fictional escape is based on the real-life flight of a woman named Mary. In the book, Eliza goes on to live in Montreal; it is said that Mary went to Chatham. Levi Coffin wrote that he visited "Eliza Harris" in 1851 in her home in Chatham, and that his wife had given her that name. Coffin is only one of many people over the past hundred and fifty years who have helped us see the strands of myth and reality that make up this famous story.

John Fairfield was a particularly brave conductor, whose tactics were so bold that Coffin tried to dissuade him from his recklessness. Fairfield would take the risk of traveling deep into the south and bringing groups of slaves away, sometimes by pretending to be their master. Originally from Virginia, he became so impressed with Ontario after one of his trips there that he moved there and continued his rescues from that base. It is believed that he brought hundreds, if not thousands, of slaves to Ontario. Laura Haviland, a schoolteacher at the Refugee Home Society (a community in Essex County), stated that he once brought twenty-seven people at one time. When he reached Ontario, the blacks there hosted a banquet at one of the churches in his honor, and a woman in her eighties or nineties began to jump around and shout praises to Jesus as she enthusiastically welcomed the refugees. Her fervent reaction was Fairfield's greatest satisfaction for the risks he had taken.

Many conductors are less well known than Fairfield and Coffin, but also took great risks. Samuel Bass was such a person. He had left Ontario and settled in Louisiana, deep in the land of slavery, because he found his wife impossible to live with. He was exceedingly fond of debating various topics, and his point of view always seemed to be the opposite of whomever he was arguing with. Yet people (other than his wife, apparently) sensed in him the sort of humor and personality that allowed him to say whatever he pleased without causing offense – even on the

Laura Smith Haviland was born in Ontario and raised in the Quaker faith. As a young woman living in Michigan she helped organize an anti-slavery society, and during her life she made several trips south as a conductor. She also served for a period as a school-teacher at the Refugee Home Society near Windsor, teaching both day and evening classes. Fugitive slaves would come from miles around to have her write letters for them to the friends they had left in the south. Before escaping, they had arranged for sympathetic whites to receive these letters, and to share the contents with those still enslaved.

subject of slavery. He boldly answered one slave-holder's comment that blacks and monkeys were not the equals of whites by replying, "I know some white men that use arguments no sensible monkey would."

Although Bass was white, his manner allowed slaves to trust him. One, Solomon Northup, overheard some of these conversations, and was emboldened to tell Bass his story over the course of several midnight meetings. Northup explained that he had been born a free man in a northern state but had been kidnapped; his "free papers" had been destroyed and he had been sold into slavery in Louisiana.

Listening to Northup's woes, Bass reflected that he was getting older and his time was getting shorter. When he died there would be no one to mourn him, or to recall any good he might have done. He resolved to secure Northup's freedom, and to leave a legacy worth remembering. He sent letters to the north, asking for documents from those who had known Northup as a free man, and eventually – after twelve long years of slavery – Solomon Northup was free to go home to his family.

However, the majority of those involved in the Underground Railroad were not white but black. A white abolitionist, James Birney, made that clear: "Such matters are almost universally managed by the colored people."

Josiah Henson was a slave who escaped to Ontario. In the 1849 edition of his autobiography, *The Life of Josiah Henson, Formerly a Slave*, he paints a picture of arriving out of the forest and taking a look at the city of Sandusky – the plain, the houses, and a ship. He spoke to a group of men and got a job carrying bags of corn onto the ship. One of them introduced him to the captain, who agreed to take the fugitive family to Buffalo, but warned them to beware of Kentucky spies who watched the harbor. To avoid Henson and his family being caught, the captain waited until dark, and then sent a small rowboat to carry them to Canada. Henson was amazed that, when they reached the Ontario shore, the crew gave him and his family three cheers to welcome them to freedom. He always remembered the name – Burnham – of the captain, who, after landing in Buffalo, put the family onto a ferryboat on their way to Waterloo and gave him a dollar as well. He also kept the memory of that morning of October 28, 1830, when he first set foot on Canadian soil. The feeling was so overwhelming that he threw himself to the ground, hugged his wife and children, and jumped around, telling an amused observer that *he was free!*

Henson soon decided that freedom was too great a gift to be hoarded. He resolved to share this treasure with others, by making risky trips back to the south. In all, he led 118 others out of bondage – and this would be only one part of his contribution to Ontario's black history. (Many people believe that the character "Uncle Tom" of *Uncle Tom's Cabin* – who dies a slave in the book – was based on Henson.)

A less well-known former slave who has been largely overlooked for his heroic work is John Mason. Having escaped from Kentucky to Canada, Mason forfeited his own security to go back and help 265 slaves escape within one space of just nineteen months. One of Mason's friends estimated that in total about 1,300 owed their freedom to Mason. During one of these daring rescues, Mason was caught on the wrong side of the Ohio River. The slave-hunters beat him terribly, breaking both of his arms in the fray. He was returned to his original master, who in turn sold him to the slave market of New Orleans. Within a year and a half, however, Mason wrote to a friend from Hamilton, Ontario, to let him know that, now that he had tasted freedom, it was impossible for him to remain a slave.

Another escaped slave who risked his own freedom to help others was Frederick Douglass – the famous abolitionist and newspaper editor, and the foremost North American black leader of the nineteenth century. Douglass writes in his autobiography that because of his location in Rochester, as well as his notoriety, he was very naturally the conductor and station-master at that city. This was particularly perilous for him because of his stature in the anti-slavery movement. Douglass was a realist; he understood that the evil institution of slavery could not be corrected by helping escaping slaves, a few at a time. It was "like an attempt to bail out the ocean with a teaspoon." Still, he claimed that nothing was more rewarding. He hid as many as eleven slaves at one time at his home. It was difficult and time-consuming to raise enough money to send them across the lake, but they patiently waited, asking for little in the way of food or comfort.

Douglass did not have to work alone. He tells of hearing

from a lawyer that a slave-master was in the city, getting the necessary papers together to arrest three young fugitives in order to return them to Maryland. The fugitives had taken the precaution of writing to their master and having the letter postmarked in Canada, but they had made the mistake of placing the word "Rochester" at the beginning of the letter, along with the date, which tipped the master off to the fact that they were still in the United States. The men were concealed in three different hiding-places. Thanks to the lawyer's warning, three conductors were sent on horseback to gather the runaways and get them aboard a ship, and safely across Lake Ontario to Toronto.

So many fugitives were coming through Rochester at the time that Douglass was forced to appeal to his friends in England, asking them to raise funds to help cover the expenses of getting them to Canada. Fortunately, the British supporters were happy to oblige.

Overshadowing even Frederick Douglass's accomplishments in helping slaves escape was William Still, the chairman of the General Vigilance Committee of Philadelphia. Under his leadership, this committee developed a web of conductors and safe houses (stations) that is the most recognized example of the sophisticated, organized network known as the Underground Railroad. Still's network alone would help close to eight hundred refugees to freedom. Still, who had taken a tour of Ontario in 1855, kept a detailed record of those helped, and published it a few years after the American Civil War under the title *The Underground Railroad*. Because of the many details it contains, his book is the most valuable first-hand account we have of this chapter in history. Most important, this book brings to life the experiences of both the passengers and the conductors. In this way, the tribute given to all the people working within the Underground Railroad is balanced by due recognition of the enormous role individuals played in their own escapes.

LETTERS.   **41**

When it is possible I wish you would advise me two days before a shipment of your intention, as Napoleon is not always on hand to look out for them at short notice. In special cases you might advise me by Telegraph, thus : " One M. (or one F.) this morning. W. S." By which I shall understand that one Male, or one Female, as the case may be, has left Phila. by the 6 *o'clock train*—one or more, also, as the case may be.
Aug. 17th, 1855.   Truly Yours, S. H. GAY.

LETTER FROM JOHN H. HILL, A FUGITIVE, APPEALING IN BEHALF OF A POOR SLAVE IN PETERSBURG, VA.

HAMILTON, Sept. 15th, 1856.

DEAR FRIEND STILL :—I write to inform you that Miss Mary Wever arrived safe in this city. You may imagine the happiness manifested on the part of the two lovers, Mr. H. and Miss W. I think they will be married as soon as they can get ready. I presume Mrs. Hill will commence to make up the articles to-morrow. Kind Sir, as all of us is concerned about the welfare of our enslaved brethren at the South, particularly our friends, we appeal to your sympathy to do whatever is in your power to save poor Willis Johnson from the hands of his cruel master. It is not for me to tell you of his case, because Miss Wever has related the matter fully to you. All I wish to say is this, I wish you to write to my uncle, at Petersburg, by our friend, the Capt. Tell my uncle to go to Richmond and ask my mother whereabouts this man is. The best for him is to make his way to Petersburg; that is, if you can get the Capt. to bring him. He have not much money. But I hope the friends of humanity will not withhold their aid on the account of money. However we will raise all the money that is wanting to pay for his safe delivery. You will please communicate this to the friends as soon as possible.
Yours truly,   JOHN H. HILL.

LETTER FROM J. BIGELOW, ESQ.

WASHINGTON, D. C., June 22d, 1854.

MR. WILLIAM STILL :—*Sir*—I have just received a letter from my friend, Wm. Wright, of York Sulphur Springs, Pa., in which he says, that by writing to you, I may get some information about the transportation of some *property* from this neighborhood to your city or vicinity.

A person who signs himself Wm. Penn, lately wrote to Mr. Wright, saying he would pay $300 to have this service performed. It is for the conveyance of *only one* SMALL package; but it has been discovered since, that the removal cannot be so safely effected without taking *two larger* packages with it. I understand that the *three* are to be brought to this city and stored in safety, as soon as the forwarding merchant in Philadelphia shall say he is ready to send on. The storage, etc., here, will cost a trifle, but the $300 will be promptly paid for the whole service. I think Mr. Wright's daughter, Hannah, has also seen you. I am also known to Prof. C. D. Cleveland, of your city. If you answer this promptly, you will soon hear from Wm. Penn himself.
Very truly yours,   J. BIGELOW.

LETTER FROM HAM & EGGS, SLAVE (U. G. R. R. AG'T).

PETERSBURG, VA., Oct. 17th, 1860.

MR. W. STILL:—*Dear Sir*—I am happy to think, that the time has come when we no doubt can open our correspondence with one another again. Also I am in hopes, that these few lines may find you and family well and in the enjoyment of good health. as it leaves me and family the same. I want you to know, that I feel as much determined to work in this glorious cause, as ever I did in all of my life, and I have some very good

William Still made a personal mission of collecting the stories of fugitive slaves, many of whom could not read or write. Thanks to him, they can still speak to us across the years, in their own words.

Still reprinted many letters, including two that he received from Isaac Forman, whom he had assisted in being sent from Virginia to Toronto. In the first letter Forman expresses his sincere appreciation for the help he has received. He has by this time a job working in a hotel, where he is making his own money and reports that he likes it very well; he closes by asking if anything can be done to help his wife, who remains enslaved.

Three months later, Forman sent another letter, with a much different tone.

> Mr. W. Still: – Dear Sir –
> . . . My soul is vexed, my troubles inexpressible, I often feel as if I were willing to die. . . . I must see my wife in short, if not, I will die. What I would not give no tongue can utter. . . . The thought of being a slave again is miserable. I hope heaven will smile upon me again, before I am one again. I will leave Canada again shortly, but I don't name the place that I go, it may be in the bottom of the ocean. If I had known as much before I left, as I do now, I would never have left until I could have found means to have brought her with me. You have never suffered from being absent from a wife, as I have. I consider that to be nearly superior to death. . . . I am determined to see her, if I die the next moment, I can say I was once happy . . . because what is freedom to me, when I know that my wife is in slavery. . . .
> I remain evermore your obedient servant,
> I. Forman

Part of the Underground Railroad that Still helped develop included Hiram Wilson, who was one of the most dedicated and remarkable conductors in Ontario. Wilson's letters to Still acknowledged the safe arrival of some of the passengers to St. Catharines. Even though Wilson occasionally did not have even

Other tales of slavery and escape were preserved by Rev. Mitchell. Because Mitchell was born free and was only half black – his mother was native – he was legally exempt from slavery. But after being orphaned at a young age he was apprenticed to a planter in North Carolina, and labored alongside slaves for many years before becoming a missionary. Mitchell was eventually sent to Toronto, to minister to black fugitives there.

enough money to pay for the postage of the letters, he made assurances that he would share anything he had with the fugitives "to the last crumb."

St. Catharines, C.W. Mar 4th, 1851

Dear Bros. Whipple
. . . A few days since a poor man just from slavery called on us whose feet were in a shocking state, having been since

about Christmas on his way between Utica & Syracuse. He hardly dared speak to people white or colored, lest he should be betrayed & taken back again to Maryland.

His right foot was badly swollen & raw like fresh cut beef & some of the bones had come out of his toes. We deeply sympathised with him, clothed him from head to foot & procured for him proper medical aid. He was very gratified for what we had done for him & gave us a brief history of himself & of his sufferings in slavery which was truly affecting. While speaking of his poor father who, 15 years ago was sold off to Georgia, to be seen of him no more & of his sisters 14 in number who were victims of the horrible slave trade & carried off to the south to be forever separated from him & from one another & of his aged mother, who died six months ago in Maryland supposed to be about 100 years of age, he sobbed & wept freely.

Poor forlorn stranger; with tears he told my wife that he never yet had found a home on earth, but said he hoped bye & bye to find a home in Heaven. . . .

Affectionately yours in the gospel & love of Jesus,
Hiram Wilson

Reverend William King had similar stature to Josiah Henson and Hiram Wilson in the Canadian anti-slavery movement. In 1853, after visiting Harriet Beecher Stowe in Andover, King learned of the abduction of a fugitive slave in Boston. Dick Sims had paid $60 to a sailor to assist him in stowing away on a ship from Georgia and had successfully reached the free state of Massachusetts. However, once in port the sailor had refused to let Sims off the ship, and had telegraphed Sims' master as to their location. The betrayer hoped to receive a reward from the master to add to the money he had already been given by the slave. Word of this treachery spread quickly. William Lloyd Garrison and Wendell Phillips, two of the most prominent abolitionists in the United States, took the necessary legal steps to have Sims removed from the ship and taken before a court of law. Sims was temporarily freed but faced a trial that might see him sent back to his owner.

Before the court case could be heard, though, Boston's Abolitionist Vigilance Committee – headed by the American abolitionist Samuel Gridley Howe and Sims' defense lawyer, Wendell Phillips – stepped in. The committee arranged for Sims to accompany the Reverend King to Canada, posing as King's servant. The two men took the train to the Ontario border. However, telegrams had been received there warning detectives to stop the train and search it before it crossed the suspension bridge to Canada. They were too late. Sensing that problems might lie ahead, the men had switched trains and got off at Niagara Falls. Waiting until nightfall, they walked across the bridge over the Niagara River, and Sims was a free man.

While the Quakers striving for abolition believed in justice and freedom for all races, their religion was also strongly pacifist (peace-loving), opposed to violent means, however desirable the end might be. John Brown, an anti-slavery activist, stood out in sharp contrast. He has been described as having all the intensity of an Old Testament prophet. Unlike most abolitionists, he believed that slavery would only come to an end after blood was shed – and he personally would use whatever methods he felt were necessary to make that happen.

In December of 1859, Brown was approached by a slave from Missouri who told him that he, his wife, and his two children, as well as another man, were to be sold within a couple of days. The slave begged Brown for help in preventing this. Brown divided his supporters into two groups, and they rode from Kansas into Missouri. They surrounded the buildings where the slaves were

John Brown was relentless in his passion to defeat slavery. He traveled across Ontario seeking supporters for his plan to establish a safe haven for blacks. In 1859 he raided a U.S. Army weapons depot in Harper's Ferry, Virginia, trying to acquire weapons to defend what he hoped would become an independent homeland in the mountains, where slaves could find shelter. The raid was doomed to failure, with several men killed on both sides. Brown himself was captured and hanged for treason and murder. He remained unrepentant to the end, writing that he was "now quite certain that the crimes of this guilty, land: will never be purged away; but with blood." His death made him a martyr in the cause of abolition, and won him the admiration of blacks across North America.

held captive and liberated them. They also freed six slaves at two neighboring plantations. In the process, they captured two white men and took some property belonging to the masters. Unfortunately, one of the owners was killed in the confrontation. In Brown's estimation, the freedom of eleven slaves was worth the death of one owner. Pursued by a posse for part of the way, Brown and his group proceeded through Kansas, Nebraska, Iowa, Illinois, and Michigan, occasionally receiving help from Underground Railroad agents along the way. The slaves were finally sent by ferry from Detroit to Windsor, where they could peacefully settle together. The trip had covered eleven hundred miles (1,800 km) and had taken eighty-two days.

Along the way, a twelfth fugitive had been added to the group: one of the rescued slaves had given birth to a son. She named him John Brown.

Unlike some abolitionists who were not necessarily convinced of the equality of the races, John Brown welcomed blacks as friends, even to sit at his family table. One of the people he greatly admired was Harriet Tubman, whom he described as "one of the best and one of the bravest persons on the continent." Gerrit Smith, who was himself a giant in the abolitionist movement, paid homage to Tubman with these words: "Nearly all the nation over, she has been heard of for her wisdom, integrity, patriotism, and bravery. The cause of freedom owes her much. The country owes her much."

Harriet Tubman was unique in the courage and dedication she displayed in helping slaves escape. Born into slavery herself, she had experienced the cruelties first-hand. She had received many floggings; she had witnessed the sale of her sisters. Her determination to change her situation is reflected in her words "There's two things I've got a right to and these are Death or Liberty. One or the other I mean to have."

Harriet Tubman found her right to liberty in St. Catharines. However, after the euphoria of her escape began to subside, she felt like "a stranger in a strange land" without her family and friends around her. Over the next several years she would rectify that by making many trips to the south; legend suggests that she rescued close to three hundred others from slavery. As her exploits became known, the reward for her capture reached $12,000 – an incredible sum at that time. She was famous for the fearless way she conducted her missions, threatening to shoot

Harriet Tubman became known as "Moses," like the biblical hero who led the Jews out of slavery and into the Promised Land. Try to imagine this prim-looking woman shepherding her charges through the dark, hiding them in chimneys and haystacks, driving them forward at gunpoint if need be. "I think slavery is the next thing to hell," she declared.

anyone who was faint of heart and did not want to go farther. She was able to boast that she "never lost a passenger."

Among the people Tubman rescued was Henry. He had made his first escape after his master had died. Although he and his family had been promised that, if they were faithful servants, they would get their freedom under the terms of their owner's will, this turned out not to be true. The family hid for some six to eight months, and during this time runaway-slave advertisements were posted for their capture. Henry's father, who lived in another county, tried unsuccessfully to arrange Underground Railroad assistance for his children, but they were forced to return to their master's widow. A year later, they were about to be sold when Harriet, who was then in Pennsylvania, heard about their situation. She came to rescue them but they could not summon the courage to leave with her. They soon regretted their decision, as rumors began again that they were to be sold. Tubman returned, and this time Henry and nine other fugitives accompanied her back to Canada.

Henry was Harriet Tubman's brother. She would later return yet again, to rescue their aged parents.

An admirer paid tribute to Tubman's extraordinary exploits:

ROCHESTER, August 29, 1868.
DEAR HARRIET: . . . You ask for what you do not need when you call upon me for a word of commendation. I need such words from you far more than you can need them from me, especially where your superior labors and devotion to the cause of the lately enslaved of our land are known as I know them. The difference between us is very marked. Most that I have done and suffered in the service of our cause has been in public, and I have received much encouragement at every step of the way. You on the other hand have labored in a private way. I have wrought in the day – you in the night. I have had the applause of the crowd and the satisfaction that comes of being approved by the multitude, while the most that you have done has been witnessed by a few trembling, scarred, and foot-sore bondmen and women, whom you have led out of the house of bondage, and whose heartfelt "God bless you" has been your only reward. . . .
Your friend,
FREDERICK DOUGLASS.

9

DESPERATE MEASURES

"I'll go to the end of the world, I will!"

These days, a century and a half after the emancipation of American slaves, it's hard to imagine the bitterness and rage that the issue raised on both sides.

The slave-owning states had built their whole economy on slave labor. If plantation owners lost their slaves, they would likely lose their estates, their grand homes, the fine futures they were planning for their sons and daughters. With all this at stake, they could persuade themselves of the rightness of the system they had known all their lives.

For abolitionists the immorality of slavery was clear, yet – outrageously – the law forbade them to work against this evil regime. Ever since the first Fugitive Slave Act, passed way back in 1793, it had been illegal to help slaves escape.

As the two sides grew farther apart, with some of the southern states threatening to break away and become independent, the government struggled to appease the slave-owners and hold the country together. That was the reason for the second Fugitive

Slave Act, passed in 1850. Now – no matter how much you detested slavery, no matter how vicious and ungodly you thought it was, you were required by law to *cooperate* in catching runaways and sending them back to a life of misery. There were punishments of fines or jail sentences for anyone who did not comply.

In the past, blacks who reached the northernmost states – whether they were legally free, or runaways pretending to be free – had felt some small measure of security. They had not been entirely safe from the cruelties and lies of slave-hunters, but most had managed to get on with their lives. Now they had no security at all. Magistrates who heard cases of alleged runaway slaves were given ten dollars if they ruled for the owner, and only five dollars if they ruled that the accused was not a slave. Blacks were not allowed to testify on their own behalf. There were many cases of free blacks, some whose families had been free for generations, being kidnapped and sold to the south because they were unable to prove their status. All this caused a flood of both fugitive slaves and free blacks fleeing into Canada. Panic-stricken, entire communities moved across the border. Some people bravely stayed behind, determined to help defend those who were accused, whether or not they were legally free.

Even prior to the passage of the 1850 Fugitive Slave Act, some abolitionists did not stand idly by when a threat was made. Thornton and Lucie Blackburn, who had escaped from Kentucky and settled in Detroit, were discovered and arrested as fugitive slaves. Their arrest sparked the first race riot in Detroit, when an angry crowd (including blacks from Ontario) rescued Thornton and got him safely over the Detroit River. Lucie was able to join her husband thanks to a particularly daring rescue by two women who had come to visit her in jail. One of the women exchanged clothes with the prisoner, who then walked out with her face covered, pretending to be weeping. By the time the ruse was discovered, Lucie was safely in the hands of friends. The

Born a slave in Virginia, Anthony Burns escaped to Boston but was arrested under the Fugitive Slave Act. Despite abolitionist uprisings of support, he was returned to slavery and sold to a planter in North Carolina. Within a year, however, a minister in Boston raised enough money to buy his freedom. Burns enrolled in college and became a pastor himself, and took over a church in St. Catharines in 1860. He died just two years later, of an illness he had acquired in inclement weather while struggling to free his church from debt.

couple were briefly imprisoned in Sandwich, but a request that they be extradited back to the United States to stand trial was rejected by the Canadians. The Blackburns eventually moved to Toronto, where they comfortably spent the rest of their lives.

Nelson Hackett was not as fortunate. Although he escaped from Arkansas in 1841, and managed to cross the border and get as far as Chatham, he was discovered there by his owner, and beaten. Then his owner had him arrested, charged with stealing possessions, including a horse, during his escape. Hackett was extradited back to the United States. This enraged anti-slavery people across Ontario – including the black citizens of Hamilton, who had sent in a petition against extradition with 178 signatures. The people of Hamilton were especially furious because they remembered the case of Jesse Happy, four years previously. Happy had escaped from Kentucky on the back of his master's horse, but he had had the foresight to leave the horse on the

Adam Crosswhite, who so barely escaped being dragged back into slavery.

American side of the border, and had sent instructions to his master on where to retrieve it. Unlike Hackett, Happy was set free from jail, since this showed that he had only borrowed the horse to secure his freedom, and was not really a horse thief. Nelson Hackett had no way to prove that he had been doing the same thing.

Adam and Sarah Crosswhite had also escaped from Kentucky, in 1843, and had settled in Michigan. When the son and nephew of their owner, along with a deputy sheriff and others, demanded that Adam come with them so he could be tried for being a runaway, Adam agreed that he would go "but not at that time of the morning." Suspecting that the couple planned to resist, the accusers told Sarah that they would leave her and Adam in peace if she would give them her children. She replied that she had already given the best years of her life as a slave, and that she would keep her children with her so they could provide for her in her old age. Word of the crisis quickly spread in the neighborhood and a crowd of both blacks and whites assembled to prevent the family from being dragged away. The Crosswhite family was able to escape through Detroit to Chatham, but some of those who had helped them were arrested, and fined for their participation in this illegal act of humanity.

In 1851 there was a more serious incident near Christiana, Pennsylvania. Led by William Parker, who was himself a fugitive slave, a group of blacks organized themselves to prevent the capture of any blacks who were threatened with return to the south. The group was kept busy at this because they were close to the slave state of Maryland. On one occasion, they were determined to prevent the capture of three fugitives by their owner and a posse of others. The owner declared that he would either get his property or have his "breakfast in hell." A fight ensued, with guns and any other available weapon, including farm implements. With bullets flying around her, Parker's wife, Eliza, blew a horn from an upper window to summon the neighbors to their aid. The master was killed and his son was badly wounded. The main participants in this "Christiana Riot" knew there was no place in the United States where they would be safe from revenge. With the help of William Still, Frederick Douglass, and others, they were able to reach Lake Ontario, where they escaped on board a steamer to Kingston. From there they traveled to Toronto and on to Windsor, finally settling at Buxton. Their wives were temporarily jailed in Pennsylvania, but were released after two months and were able to join their husbands.

In what became known as "the Jerry rescue," William "Jerry" McHenry was captured in October 1851, in Syracuse, New York. A crowd of blacks went to the courtroom, grabbed the fugitive slave, and made an attempt to escape. Officers soon overcame them and Jerry was retaken. Not to be deterred, a large group stormed the jail and fought the police. This time they made good the rescue, and McHenry was safely forwarded to Kingston.

In 1851, the year of the "Christiana Riot" and the "Jerry rescue," there was a substantial black community in Sandwich. That was when the Baptist congregation, which had been meeting for over ten years, erected this chapel. It is still in use today.

However, he was not the only one who had to go to Ontario to find a safe haven. Fourteen whites and twelve blacks were charged with breaking the law under the Fugitive Slave Act. Nine of the blacks, including Jarmain Loguen, fled to Canada to avoid being tried. Welcomed into the home of Hiram Wilson, Loguen continued his anti-slavery activities from the northern side of the border.

Joshua Glover, who had escaped from Missouri, had a similar experience after reaching Wisconsin in 1854. While playing cards in his shanty (shed home) he was taken by surprise and over-powered by two deputy marshals who broke in, and clubbed and handcuffed. While he was in jail in Milwaukee, a mob broke into the jail, seized Glover, and sent him to Ontario via the Underground Railroad. He safely found his way to Toronto, but some of those who assisted in his escape were fined and imprisoned.

Even people who escaped to Ontario were not always safe from their owners' attempts to retrieve their property. Reverend

John "Daddy" Hall was born in Amherstburg in 1807, to black and native parents, but he, his mother, and ten siblings were captured by American slave-hunters and carried into bondage in Kentucky. Hall grew up there and married, but he and his wife eventually escaped to Canada. He lived in Toronto and Durham, and then became the first black to settle in what is now Owen Sound. It is believed that when he died he was 118 years old.

King from Buxton stated that "Sometimes the planters would come into the settlement and converse with slaves that had escaped from them, and try to get them to go back with them, promising to be kind to them in the future and to forgive the past, but they were never able to persuade any of them to return south." Daniel Ducket's owner had a different tactic. Someone whom Ducket had met in Michigan, whom he thought to be a friend, accompanied him to Canada. The "friend" – in fact a slave-hunter who was anxious for a reward – tried unsuccessfully to lure Ducket back to Michigan, where his owner could seize him. Seeing that this plan would not work, the bounty hunter settled for stealing one of Ducket's horses and taking it to Michigan, knowing that the runaway slave could not follow him to reclaim his horse without being captured and returned to slavery.

Those who lived closest to the border had to be the most vigilant. Slavery had had such an effect on Joseph Sanford of Windsor that, despite years of freedom, he still did not feel secure. Even at the age of sixty-five, he clung to a superstitious belief that slave-holders had a sort of magical power they could wield to make slaves do their bidding. Upon hearing that his previous master was staying in Amherstburg, Sanford refused to spend the night in his own home, fearing that the man would use his "charms" to lure him back to the south.

One brother and sister escaped to Ontario, but their owner valued them so much that he hired a top slave-catcher to help get them back. The pursuers arranged for a network of spies to watch the Lake Erie ports from Cleveland to Buffalo. The conductors of the Underground Railroad were aware of this surveillance, so they arranged for the siblings to dress as sailors, and to pretend to be crew members on one of the finest side-wheel steamers on the lakes. As fate would have it, the master and slave-catcher decided to give up the chase as fruitless, and boarded that very ship to return to the south. While on board, they recognized the fugitives and told the captain that they would pay him handsomely if he would stop at any American port before they reached Detroit, and allow them to leave. He agreed – but he ordered the ship to first pull into Amherstburg, on the Canadian side, to take on firewood. The slave-owner was incensed, and offered the captain $1,000 to land in Michigan first. The captain replied that he would only keep his promise to let the owner disembark in Michigan.

As you might expect, the two slaves bounded off the ship at Amherstburg, with the slave-owner and slave-catcher in hot pursuit. The people of Amherstburg "roughly handled" the pursuers, enough that they were glad to find safety back on board the ship as they continued on their way, empty-handed, back to Kentucky.

Daniel Payne was another Kentucky slave-owner who discovered the danger of trying to take by force what Canada would not allow by law. Three of his escaped slaves, brothers, successfully crossed the border. Payne discovered them several months later, and tried to lure them back with the promise that he would give them their manumission papers and pay them for their labor. After they refused his offer, he sought the assistance of a black man who invited the fugitives to come to a dance in Detroit. Correctly suspecting that this was just another trick, the slaves decided to develop a ruse of their own.

They devised a plan to send word that one of the brothers was ill and lying in the barracks at Windsor. When Payne tried to seize the opportunity of recovering his weakened "property," he was rushed by a group of men who tied him up and stripped him. Borrowing a plantation slave-whip that Henry Bibb had kept as a reminder of sadder days, the brothers proceeded to give their owner the same number of lashes that they had witnessed him apply to their mother's naked back. Following that, they returned his clothes and sent him on his way, back across the Detroit River.

Charles and William Baby, of Sandwich, employed a young man named Andrew who admitted to being a runaway slave. Six months after they hired him, a man who had the dress and manner of a southern planter knocked on their door. He declared that Andrew was his property, and that the slave had stolen his horse, Sweepstakes, when making his escape. He offered $2,000 for the return of his slave, but the Baby brothers refused.

When they talked to Andrew, he admitted taking the horse but insisted that he had released it so it could find its way home. After that, he said, agents of the Underground Railroad had helped him reach Canada.

The planter was sent away without his slave, but he swore that this would not be the end of the affair. Andrew was afraid,

This painting, called "A Ride for Liberty – The Fugitive Slaves," is said to be based on a real escape witnessed by the painter, Eastman Johnson. But most escapes were much slower and more physically demanding. A black family sharing a horse would be suspected immediately, and – as Nelson Hackett, Andrew, Solomon Moseby, and many other fugitives discovered – the horse itself could cause no end of trouble.

not only for himself but also for the brothers who were giving him shelter. At night, the young man locked himself in an upper room with two guns for protection.

A few Sundays later, when he assumed the brothers would be at church, the planter returned with five other men to help in a kidnapping. Andrew resisted them with an ax handle, and "went at them with the will of a tiger." The noise from the ruckus attracted "a cavalcade of horse carts and cavalry men hastening home from church." The would-be kidnappers made a hasty exit back to their boat, and hurried across the Detroit River. Since it was obviously not safe for Andrew to remain so close to the

The Niagara jail and courthouse, built in 1817 – scene of the bloody Moseby rescue.

American border, a fund was established to raise money, and he was sent by stagecoach to the safety of Toronto.

Like Andrew, Solomon Moseby was from Kentucky and had used his master's horse to make his escape. When he was discovered living in Niagara, his owner knew that he could not be extradited from Canada on the grounds that he was an escaped slave, so Moseby was arrested and charged with horse theft. The governor of Kentucky agreed with this legal tactic and demanded that the slave be returned for punishment. A huge crowd of blacks from the Niagara district were determined that Solomon would not be sent back into slavery and perhaps to his death. They surrounded the jail, and rushed the sheriff and the military guards when the handcuffed Moseby was led out. The slave was successfully rescued. Tragically, two other blacks were killed in the rescue.

Although men were the traditional fighters and defenders, women facing the evils of slave-hunting often mounted a daring defense. In the Moseby case they had encouraged their men to carry no weapons, and to attempt to make the rescue without violence. However, when violence did erupt, the women were at the center of the fray, placing themselves between black men and white in the belief that the guards would be less likely to harm females. One woman held the sheriff pinned. Another contemptuously prevented a soldier from firing his gun by knocking the barrel aside, and then holding him in such a way that he could not shoot. The woman who was said to have been a leading spirit in all of this was interviewed soon after the event, by Anna Jameson, an Englishwoman living in Canada. Mrs. Jameson was particularly intrigued by the female involvement and bravery in the rescue, and later published her observations in book form.

She was a fine creature, apparently about five-and-twenty, with a kindly animated countenance; but the feelings of exasperation and indignation had evidently not yet subsided. She told us, in answer to my close questioning, that she had formerly been a slave in Virginia; that so far from being ill-treated, she had been regarded with especial kindness by the family on whose estate she was born. When she was about sixteen her master died, and it was said that all the slaves on the estate would be sold, and therefore she ran away.

"Were you not attached to your mistress?" I asked.

"Yes" said she, "I like my mistress, but I did not like to be sold."

I asked her if she was happy here in Canada?

She hesitated a moment, and then replied, on my repeating the question, "Yes – that is, I was happy here – but now – I don't know – I thought we were safe here – I thought that nothing could touch us here, on your British ground, but it seems I was mistaken, and if so I won't stay here – I won't – I won't! I'll go and find some country where they cannot reach us! I'll go to the end of the world, I will!"

10

HARD TIMES IN A HARD LAND

". . . we have to row against the wind and tide . . ."

Although many slaves seeking freedom looked upon Canada as the place where the Underground Railroad ended and freedom, security, and opportunity began, the reality could be very different. While it was true that the code of laws offered protection against injustice and oppression, the administration of those laws was not color-blind. No matter what legislation decreed equal rights, personal prejudices and discrimination often ruled. One common thread that linked the words and thoughts of many blacks across the province was that their presence was generally tolerated but seldom welcomed. Interviews conducted at the time often expressed the observation that prejudice was more insidious in Canada than south of the border, even in the southern states. Those interviewed argued that, at the very least, in the United States there were no illusions as to their place in society. Samuel Gridley Howe maintained that Canadians had no right to charge the United States with the sin of prejudice, when they had their own fair share.

Despite the fact that blacks had fought and died for their country, they seldom shared in the rewards for patriotism. Black loyalists who had fought in the armies and militias and had been promised land sometimes found that their lots were smaller and less desirable than those granted to their fellow soldiers of European ancestry. One such group from Niagara submitted a request that they be granted a parcel of property where they could all live together "separate from the white settlers," so that they could support each other. The request was not successful. Veterans of military conflicts after the American Revolution experienced similar problems. Residents within the Queen's Bush argued that they had been promised land for fighting in the colored militia during the Rebellion of 1837, and they had done the backbreaking work of making the land useful for farming, and it was now being sold out from under them.

Colonel John Prince, who had welcomed blacks during the 1837 Rebellion, had a change of heart twenty years later. Now a Member of Parliament, he publicly voiced his opinions in response to a meeting of blacks in Toronto who had censured him. On the one hand, he bragged, "I assert, without fear of contradiction, that I have been the friend – the only friend of our Western 'Darkies' for more than twenty years." Apparently he was weak on the definition of friendship, for he continued, "It has been my misfortune, and the misfortune of my family to live among those Blacks." In one of the strange contradictions that are so common in matters of race relations, Prince two years later hosted between 1,200 and 1,500 people at his farm to celebrate the August 1 anniversary of the 1834 emancipation of blacks in Canada.

Many others shared Prince's anti-black sentiments. Samuel Ringgold Ward, who had participated in the "Jerry rescue," was forced to flee to Canada. He expressed his anger at being denied a cabin on a boat because he was black in a letter to Henry Bibb,

A family dressed in their Sunday finery.

for publication in his newspaper, *The Voice of the Fugitive.*
Embittered by his experiences on both sides of the border, Ward
made the point that any claim that there was no prejudice in
Canada was "about as empty as the Yankees boast of democracy."

A document signed in 1849 by many white men in Kent
County seemed to confirm the accuracy of Ward's feelings.
When there was a proposal to create a black settlement in the
county, the synod (local ruling body) of the Presbyterian Church
received a petition objecting to the plan, and declaring, in most
un-Christian terms, that:

> The Negro is a distinct species of the Human Family and, in
> the opinion of your Memorialists is far inferior to that of the
> European. Let each link in the great Scale of existence have its
> place; the White man was never intended to be linked with

the Black. Amalgamation is as disgusting to the Eye, as it is immoral in its tendencies and all good men will discountenance it.

Those feelings ran throughout the province. In the classic 1852 memoir *Roughing It in the Bush*, Susanna Moodie refers to Tom Smith, a runaway slave who settled near Peterborough prior to 1834. He set up a barbershop and also did laundry for the townspeople. His good-natured, civil disposition won over even some of the most prejudiced people – at least, until he took an Irish girl for his bride. The neighbors were indignant at what they considered to be an insult to propriety. Some of the young men decided to punish Smith by breaking into his house and dragging him out of bed and outside into the winter's night. They "rode him upon a rail" – a humiliating and painful punishment in which he was tied straddling a narrow piece of wood, and paraded around. He was abused so severely that he died. Then the killers abandoned his body. No one was ever arrested or charged.

Even those white people who tried to help the growing black population could suffer attacks from their fellow citizens. In 1849, James Thompson of Galt chastised a group of Canadian anti-slavery sympathizers, telling them that they were wasting their time, which would be better spent taking care of the poor people of their own race, and enthusiastically giving his opinion that black people were "a nuisance wherever they go, no one can trust them they steal and they are lazy." He suggested that they "turn your attention to something more honourable."

Amelia M. Murray, who traveled throughout Ontario in 1854, agreed with Thompson. Her observation was that "One of the evils consequent upon Southern Slavery, is the ignorant and miserable set of coloured people who throw themselves into Canada. . . . I must regret that the well-meant enthusiasm of the Abolitionists has been without judgment."

The schoolhouse of St. Andrew's Church, in Niagara. Black children had to use a roughly furnished upstairs room. "Oh, it was full – full of children," recalled one student. "The benches were slabs with the flat side up and the bark of the tree down, with round sticks put in slanting for legs. The children all studied aloud and the one that made the most noise was the best scholar...."

There was a very serious disagreement between the races on the subject of integrated schools. Education held special promise to parents who had been denied the opportunity to learn to read while they had been enslaved. They recognized that any chance of their children achieving the goals they themselves could only dream about hinged on receiving a good education. In most areas of the province, though, black children were denied entry into the district schools. Missionaries and blacks who had been able to attend school in some of the northern U.S. states became

teachers in segregated schools, but these usually lacked sufficient
funds to pay the teachers and to purchase necessary supplies.

The Bloomfield school, near Chatham, made a less than satisfactory compromise on the issue of integration. The one-room
log building where white children studied had a lean-to for the
"Negro" children attached to one side. An opening was cut
through the wall so they could see the blackboard, hear the
teacher, and, in the winter, get a little heat from the wood stove.
Also in Kent County, the Willis children – nine-year-old Charles
and his sister Maria, who was even younger – were treated so
badly by the other children that they were forced to leave the
school. Then they were permanently expelled for being absent.
Refusing a five-dollar bribe to keep them away, their father –
whose taxes helped support the school – demanded that his children be allowed to attend like anyone else. He sent them back to
school, but they were refused entry.

Incidents like these showed that in some cases the blacks
really needed to establish their own schools. Years earlier, blacks
in Hamilton petitioned the government for a separate school, but
they were advised by the lieutenant-governor – in an open letter
dated September 13, 1838, in *The Bytown Gazette and Ottawa
Advertiser* – that he opposed separate schools, and that any problems that arose in the school should be brought to the attention of
the government. Some Hamiltonians even up to the time of the
Civil War maintained this ideal of no segregated schools. During
that time, the Anglican Church and a high school principal
refused to allow blacks to be excluded from classes. This was not
the case in many other areas.

The Reverend Lewis C. Chambers, who had recently relo-
cated his missionary work to in and around the Dawn settlement
(see Chapter 11), showed the indomitable optimism that many
blacks nonetheless felt about their lives in Canada. In a letter
dated November 2, 1860, to the secretary of the American

The American Missionary Association was founded in Albany, New York, in 1846, to promote mission work and Christian education. It also sent financial support to the settlements where ex-slaves were building new lives, such as the Refugee Home Society, the Dawn Settlement, and a number of other communities across Ontario. Prior to the Civil War, the AMA had missions not only in Canada and the U.S. but also in Egypt, Siam (Thailand), Haiti, Jamaica, and West Africa.

Missionary Association, which helped to subsidize his ministry, Reverend Chambers wrote that he had moved to London after spending a very brief time in Ingersoll. On September 24, the first night he arrived in Ingersoll, whites had burned his home to the ground because they did not want a black preacher. Nine days later, his oldest son, whom he described as a fine boy of about sixteen years of age, had fallen off his horse while taking it to get a drink in the Big Bear Creek and had drowned. However, the stoic Chambers began the letter by saying that both he and his family were well, and concluded it by saying that the "Lord is with us and the weather is fine."

Life often remained difficult for ex-slaves, even after they reached freedom. Consider the hard lot of Parker Joyner of

The R. Nathaniel Dett Chapel, in Niagara Falls. This BME church was founded in 1836 and is still in service. It was renamed in 1983 to honor a native-born parishioner, a renowned musician and composer of sacred music who served as the church's organist from 1898 to 1903.

Sandwich Township. Enslaved from birth to age forty-five, he had finally escaped from Norfolk, Virginia, in 1857. Accompanying him were his wife and youngest daughter; he was forced to leave his other six children behind. By 1863, the physical effects of harsh treatment during his enslavement had confined him to bed for ten months. He was unable to build a log home or even to chop wood for the winter. His wife had done the wood-chopping for the previous six years, but she was now too ill, after working in the mud and snow without proper shoes. Joyner's optimism was fading as his family was forced to ask for the charity of others.

William Mason experienced personal trouble to an even greater degree. He had successfully escaped from slavery and made his way to what was then the small town of Detroit, where he found a wife and decided to settle down to peaceful married life. Instead, he found himself worse off than before, because "his wife proved to be a veritable she devil in petticoats, with a tongue that was keener than the master's lash." When Mason could not stand any more, he ran away to Canada. His jilted wife contacted the slave-catchers and put them on the trail of her faithless husband.

The slave-hunters tracked Mason to Erie, near Niagara, and tried to physically seize him, but Mason fought back with a butcher's knife. They left for a while, and a sympathetic, prominent white man hid William so securely that they said, "Even the devil himself could not find him." The story continued with several other exciting incidents, until Mason was smuggled away and hidden under barrel staves in the hull of a ship, and successfully made his escape. Eventually he found another, more amiable wife, and made a happy home in Kingston.

Pioneer life was difficult for most people, and for blacks the challenges were particularly daunting. But most of them agreed that, difficult or not, living free in Canada was much better than the alternative. Benjamin Miller of London put it all into perspective:

> I was born in Lincoln County, North Carolina. I left there when I was twelve years old, and was brought up in Lincoln County, Missouri. I was in bondage in Missouri, too. I can't say that my treatment was bad. In one respect I say it was not bad, but in another, I consider it was as bad as could be. I was a slave. That covers it all. . . . I have done first rate here. I will tell you what I call first-rate, and then you can judge. I say first rate, from the fact that we have to row against wind and tide when we get here, and being brought up illiterate, I consider that if we live and keep our families well fed and clad, we have done first-rate.

Jim Henson, known to his neighbors in Owen Sound as Old Man Henson, had been a slave in Maryland before escaping to Pennsylvania, then to New Jersey, and finally to Canada. Nineteenth-century biographies of fugitive slaves are very rare, but Henson's fascinating recollections, first published in 1889, have recently been republished under the title Broken Shackles: Old Man Henson from Slavery to Freedom.

The loved ones left behind in slavery were never forgotten. In a poignant passage in his will, dated 1861, William Fields described himself as a yeoman (free farmer), aged forty-two, "of the Township of Raleigh in the County of Kent and the province of Canada." He bequeathed his home and his property of twenty-five acres (10 ha) first to his wife, and upon her death to his daughter, Mary Fields, "now in bondage," should she manage to come to Canada. But he could not count upon her coming to claim her inheritance; he left alternate instructions in case she could not escape slavery. Just four years later, slavery was abolished through America; Mary's father died shortly after writing his will, however, and never had the comfort of learning her fate.

However hard life may have been in Canada, it sounded just fine to at least one young white woman. An ex-slave named Kate Dudley Baumont clearly relished a scandal she recalled from earlier days.

When we lived on the Preston farm something happened that raised a lot of talk. One of the Preston girls fell in love with the Negro coachman and run off and married him in Canada. She said she never wanted to marry a white man. She never did have no white beaux as a girl.

Her father was so hurt then he said he was going to disown her; but he did give them $10,000. Then he said he never wanted them to come back to visit him or his folks, but his folks could go up to Canada and visit with her or her family.

Before the Prestons threatened to kill the man, but the girl, she said if they killed him she would kill some of them herself, too. She told them that she persuaded him to take her, and that she had been in love with him for years, and had tried ever so long to get him to run off with her and marry her. Ole Miss [Mrs. Preston] like to have died, but she got over it, and took trips up to Canada when she wanted to see her daughter. But the girl and her husband never came back to her old home.

They had a family, so we heard, and he was doing well and had some kind of business, and later, it was said, he made a lot of money. He was a nice looking man; dark, but fine featured.

11

LEARNING TO LIVE IN LIBERTY

". . . simply because they are free men."

In 1864 – the year before slavery ended in the United States – came the publication of the *Report to the Freedmen's Inquiry Commission: The Refugees from Slavery in Canada West.* This report on the living conditions of ex-slaves in Ontario, more commonly known as the Howe report, had been prepared by Samuel Gridley Howe and two other officials appointed by the U.S. Secretary of War. One of the ex-slaves they had interviewed, Mrs. Joseph Wilkinson, compared her present life to her past:

> I considered my clothes and the little things I had when in slavery my own but I didn't see it as I do now. I see now that every thing I considered mine didn't belong to me, but could be taken away from me at any time. I didn't set the same store by my little things that I do now, for I didn't see things then as I do now.

Clarice Brantford stands in front of her family home on Brock Street, in Amherstburg.

Mrs. Wilkinson had had the rare good fortune to be contented when she was a slave, and she had had a genuine affection for her owners. She had come to Ontario only to follow her husband, who had been badly treated and had escaped. Yet, though she had previously felt that she was treated "same as if I were free," it was only after she arrived that she began to grasp what freedom really meant. For many of her contemporaries, too, freedom was something they always wanted but could not fully understand until it was theirs. Missionary Benjamin Slight of Amherstburg stated that "their former bondage has shackled their minds." Harriet Tubman observed, "I grew up like a neglected weed, – ignorant of liberty, having no experience of it. . . . Now I've been free, I know what a dreadful condition slavery is." Likewise, when fifteen slaves from Louisiana were told by the abolitionist Reverend William King that they would be freed, "They seemed not to understand what was meant by going to Canada; most of them thought it was some new plantation I had purchased and I was going to take them to it. I then explained to them that Canada was a free country; that there were no slaves there. . . . The good news seemed to have little effect upon them. They had come to consider that slavery was their normal condition. They did not know what freedom meant."

No matter how slaves acquired their freedom – whether they were given it by others or took it for themselves – many knew that Canada was the place where they could truly enjoy it. There were still many unknowns and many obstacles ahead, but the experience of landing on free soil often had a magical effect. One ship captain who was bound for Buffalo picked up two fugitives in Cleveland. He ordered the ship to make a special out-of-the-way stop on the shore of Lake Erie. He was deeply touched by what happened there.

> They said, "Is this Canada?" I said, "Yes, there are no slaves in this country"; then I witnessed a scene I shall never forget. They seemed to be transformed; a new light shone in their eyes, their tongues were loosed, they laughed and cried, prayed and sang praises, fell upon the ground and kissed it, hugged and kissed each other. . . .

Harriet Tubman expressed her feelings more eloquently to her biographer, Sarah H. Bradford, author of *Scenes in the Life of Harriet Tubman.*

> When I found I had crossed that line I looked at my hands to see if I was the same person. There was such a glory over every thing; the sun came like gold through the trees, and over the fields, and I felt like I was in Heaven.

The dress and carriage of this gentleman in St. Catharine's suggest that he's a cab-driver.

Once they were past that first elation, however, most blacks had choices to make. Where would they settle? There were black communities throughout Ontario. Many people traveled to several different areas across the province, until they found the place and the situation that most suited them; their narratives often describe living temporarily in one place, and moving to another, perhaps several times. Some of those moves included temporary or permanent returns to the United States. For example, Isaac Mason moved from Montreal, to Kingston, to Toronto, before briefly working in the Queen's Bush, and then went back across the border to Massachusetts.

The majority of the blacks lived among the white population, although – like immigrants to any country – they often clustered together to form their own community within the larger one. This was true in places with large black populations, such as Windsor, Amherstburg, Chatham, London, Hamilton, St.

Catharines and Toronto, but it also applied to areas with smaller populations scattered across the province, such as around Oro Township, near Lake Simcoe. A group of people from the Sandy Lake area of Pennsylvania transplanted themselves to Grey County following the passage of the 1850 Fugitive Slave Act, so that they could maintain their sense of community in a new country. There were also black communities in Gosfield Township in Essex County, in the Brantford area near the Grand River, in Woolwich Township in Waterloo County, and farther north, in Collingwood and Owen Sound.

In addition to the black neighborhoods in larger communities, there were also several planned settlements, set up exclusively for blacks. Here, they hoped to live comfortably together, surrounded by others who shared their painful history and would be supportive in all the things that gave meaning to life.

Colonization societies had been active in the United States from the early nineteenth century, striving to create all-black settlements in various parts of the world, including Canada, the United States, Africa, and the Caribbean. Some advocates of colonization believed that it was noble to give blacks a home of their own; others simply wanted to be rid of them. Many colonizers considered Africa the place of choice. The British established a colony in Sierra Leone, on the west coast of Africa, following the American Revolution. Many ex-slaves living in Nova Scotia were transported there by ship. The American Colonization Society founded a similar colony in Liberia, just south of Sierra Leone, in 1821. Thousands of black Americans moved there, but their death rates were high from disease, farming was difficult, and the existing population resented their presence. In later years, Canadian blacks such as John Brooks, a community leader in the Queen's Bush, emigrated there as well; Brooks went to lend the skills he had developed in Ontario to the struggling African community.

The Reverend Josiah Henson and his wife, Nancy Gambril. Henson was born into slavery in Kentucky in 1789. After reaching Canada and freedom, he became a prominent abolitionist and a conductor in the Underground Railroad. He was one of the founders of the Dawn Settlement, and also established the British-American Institute, a school where ex-slaves could learn the skills they needed in their new life.

The Hensons' home in Dresden. When the family first arrived in Canada, a landowner let them live in an old shanty occupied by his pigs. Henson spent the first night clearing out the pig filth and piling up clean straw for his family to sleep on.

In 1829, the city of Cincinnati, Ohio, decided to enforce the "Ohio Black Law." This meant that although there was no slavery in Ohio, every black man would be required to pay a $500 dollar bond, and anyone who hired a black would be fined $100 – hefty sums in those days. Faced with these outrageous terms, the blacks formed a colonization society to investigate making Ontario their home. They bought property in what is now Lucan, with the financial support of American Quakers, and established the Wilberforce Settlement. James C. Brown, who was the leader of the group, estimated that four hundred and sixty people moved to various locations in Canada. Of these, about two hundred settled on the Wilberforce lands.

The Dawn Settlement, at Dresden, Ontario, was the next planned colony. The white missionary Hiram Wilson had formed a friendship with the former slave Josiah Henson while the two lived in Colchester Township, in Essex County.

An ordained Congregational minister, Wilson had come to southern Ontario in 1836 and had quickly traveled to black communities throughout the region. The American Anti-Slavery Society supported his work, paying him eight dollars per week. Much of his traveling was done on foot. He crossed the province several times in his role as a missionary, and was responsible for establishing ten schools for black children by 1839. He was also instrumental in forming several anti-slavery societies in both Ontario and the United States.

Determined to do more to make the lot of the blacks easier, Wilson asked for the help of James C. Fuller, a Quaker friend who lived in New York. Fuller raised $1,500 from sympathizers in England. After calling for blacks across Ontario to meet in London, to determine how best to use the money, in 1841 Wilson and Henson bought two hundred acres (80 ha) on which to begin a settlement. The community would surround the proposed British-American Institute, which they planned to be a

Moving to a black settlement, a family might pay a token fee to buy a farm of fifty acres (20 ha) – a daunting responsibility for people who might have no experience of general farming, and might never have owned anything before.

manual labor school. Approximately five hundred blacks settled in and around Dawn, to farm and work in local mills and other industries.

The Reverend William King was also a major contributor to the settlement movement. He gathered the support of the Governor General of Canada West, Lord Elgin, as well as the Presbyterian Church of Canada, and an interracial group of supporters and investors from across Ontario who took the name "the Elgin Association." The association acquired land in Raleigh Township, in Kent County. The community they established there – officially known as "The Elgin Settlement and Buxton Mission" but most commonly referred to as Buxton – was the largest and most successful of the planned settlements. Strict rules for settlement and self-reliance made it both a model for success and a convincing argument against the negative

Buxton Mission 1860

School House   Rev. Wm King's House   Post Office

An early sketch of the Buxton Mission, center of the Elgin Settlement. In addition to those living within the settlement's 9,000 acres (3,600 ha), hundreds more fugitive slaves and free blacks resided in the surrounding area. The main buildings clustered around the house of the founder, the Reverend William King, who had both inherited and purchased slaves in Louisiana whom he then helped reach Canada.

stereotypes that were firmly rooted in the minds of many white people. Frederick Douglass visited Buxton in August of 1854. According to the *Western Planet* newspaper of August 9, he was impressed by what he saw:

> He was proud of his race to-day, when on visiting the Elgin Association, at Buxton, he saw men, women and children, who but a short time ago, were under the rod of the slave driver, engaged in peaceful and noble pursuit of agriculture . . . administering to their own comforts, and growing in intelligence and wealth. The efficiency of the common school, where the higher branches of education are taught, and eagerly acquired, did his heart good, and filled him with hope for the future.

The Refugee Home Society, the last major settlement for fugitive slaves, was founded in 1851 by a group of abolitionists from Michigan and Ontario. Henry and Mary Bibb, who published *The Voice of the Fugitive* newspaper, were two of the agents who would carry out the administration. People in the United States made donations and supported the hundred and fifty people who moved to the 2,000 acres (800 ha) in Sandwich and Maidstone townships, in Essex County, that made up the settlement. There the new arrivals found a school for their children, a church for their comfort, and some relief from their troubles. By 1860, a young woman who four years earlier had been "a little slave girl that did not know her letters" was already teaching school there. Couples whose marriages had not been legally recognized in the south were finally able to see their union ordained by the law as well as sanctioned by God. People could also depend on a network of neighbors, stretching from Detroit to Windsor to the Society lands, who would rally almost immediately to protect their members from any visitors suspected of being slave-hunters.

Mary Ann Shadd, a young black woman who had moved to Canada when the second Fugitive Slave Act was passed, wrote a persuasive booklet entitled *Notes of Canada West*, appealing to blacks to move north across the border and find a home in Ontario, and noting their increasing desire

> to learn of the climate, soil and productions, and of the inducements offered generally to emigrants, and to them particularly, since that the passage of the odious Fugitive Slave Law has made a residence in the United States to many of them dangerous in the extreme. . . .

The entire topic of colonization of blacks outside of the United States was extremely controversial and divisive, because

Mary Ann Shadd was North America's first female newspaper editor, at The Provincial Freeman. *During her remarkable life she was also a schoolteacher and principal, a Civil War recruiter for the Union Army, and, later, a lawyer in Washington, D.C.*

many abolitionists felt that blacks should have every right of citizenship in the United States, but too often the reality was that places like Canada were the only satisfactory option. Even some of the most prominent American blacks – such as Abraham Shadd (Mary Ann's father), Martin Delany, Samuel Ringgold Ward (who for a time worked with Mary Ann on *The Provincial Freeman*), Jarmain Loguen, and many others – abolitionists, Underground Railroad operatives, and representatives from the churches and the Coloured Conventions – eventually felt compelled to move to Ontario. (Coloured Conventions were held across the northern states, beginning in 1830, so that black community leaders could meet to work out a unified approach to the problems facing their race.)

Canada hosted its own convention at St. Lawrence Hall in Toronto, in 1851, and Frederick Douglass was one of the speakers.

Both black and white delegates from across Ontario, the northern United States, England, and Jamaica came together at the urging of Henry Bibb. Resolutions were passed, including one condemning the Fugitive Slave Act, which they termed "an insult to God, and an outrage against humanity," and another praising "her Britannic Majesty's just and powerful Government, for the protection afforded us" and recommending Canada as the destination for blacks from the United States.

There was already a history of interracial cooperation in Ontario. The Upper Canada Anti-Slavery Society, founded in the 1830s, and the Anti-Slavery Society of Canada, founded in 1851, were composed of people of both African and European heritage. There were also many regional societies with similar goals. The Anti-Slavery Society of Canada became a national organization with branches in Kingston, Hamilton, Windsor, London, Grey County, and St. Catharines. The goals of these organizations were compatible with the goals of other groups and individuals who wanted to provide a home and a social structure where fugitive slaves and free blacks could build their lives.

Meeting spiritual needs was important for a people who had long depended on religious faith as their support. Missionaries lived and traveled throughout the province to try to provide this support. In the communities, however, problems sometimes developed between white missionaries and schoolteachers and the black population. In Amherstburg, for example, feelings ran high against missionary Isaac Rice. The same was true of teacher Mary Teall in the Queen's Bush, and David Hotchkiss at the Refugee Home Society. Even Hiram Wilson, who devoted much of his life to the cause, did not escape criticism. There was a gulf between the black experience and the white that could not be easily crossed. The nineteenth-century notion that blacks were less capable of managing their own affairs, that they needed direction and guidance if they hoped to prosper, persisted even among some of the most well-meaning whites of the day.

Determined, proud, and striving to further assert the independence that many had only recently achieved, the black people of Canada came together to build their own institutions. They built churches and schools, and became their own ministers and teachers. Baptist and Methodist churches sprang up almost anywhere there was even a small black settlement. Their message was not only Christian in nature, but anti-slavery as well – which was, after all, a branch of the same tree. The Amherstburg Baptist Association merged with the Canadian Anti-Slavery Baptist Association to form a union of churches in Amherstburg, Sandwich, Chatham, Mount Pleasant, Hamilton, Colchester, Buxton, New Canaan, Little River, Windsor, Dresden, Shrewsbury, Gosfield, and Puce River, as well as five Michigan cities. Toronto, Wilberforce, St. Thomas, St. Catharines, North Cayuga, and other places had at least one Baptist church. The African Methodist Episcopal Church also had a large number of churches in Canada. At a convention held in Chatham in 1856, many of these Canadian churches decided to become independent from their larger connection in the United States. They adopted the name "British Methodist Episcopal Church" (BME), partly in tribute to the government that had offered them safe sanctuary in Canada. Interestingly, some churches in Michigan and Indiana were also part of the BME.

The spirit of independence that inspired black churches, schools, and other institutions was also a foundation of the communities they built. People who had never before been free – who had followed orders and lived very limited lives – faced challenges they had never before had to deal with. There were matters of planning, of finance, of legal procedure. Those who had slaved in the fields might know little about working in the home, and vice versa. By sharing their lives, they also pooled their knowledge, and solved each others' problems.

The British Methodist Episcopal (BME) Church in Owen Sound was a spiritual center for the growing black population. The minutes of a BME conference in 1869 list thirty congregations in Canada, whose 1,400 members had to come up with the bishop's annual salary of $525.

In addition to these everyday advantages, there was another benefit of living in specific areas: there was always the chance of one of those extraordinary reunitings of families who had been separated in slavery. James and Fanny Smith, who had been split apart seventeen years earlier, had one such reunion in Sandwich:

> While traveling about among his fugitive brethren, and occasionally telling where he was originally from, [Mr. Smith] found a man who told him he knew a woman in Canada who was from near Richmond, Virginia, who had once belonged to a man there by the name of Wm. Wright, and that he sold her, &c. This of course aroused Mr. Smith's curiosity to see the woman; so he went the next day to where he had been told that she lived. As he approached the house he saw a female who he thought resembled "Fanny", his long bereft wife; and as he approached her with trembling lest he might be mistaken he offered his hand and ventured to call her by her

former name, to which she answered with astonishment. At this moment her eyes sparkled and flashed like strokes of lightning upon his furrowed cheeks and wrinkled brow, and with uplifted hands and joyful heart she exclaimed from the depths of her soul, "Oh! Is this my beloved husband who I never again expected to see?" To this appeal there was a glorious response on the part of the husband; they embraced each other in the bonds of Christian love and wept aloud for joy, and glorified God with their bodies and spirits, which are his, for his great mercy in bringing them together again on this earth, and they are now living happily together on the Queen's "Free Soil".

After 1860, when abolitionist Abraham Lincoln was elected president, eleven of the slave-owning states finally broke away to form their own country. By the summer of 1861 this rebel Confederacy was locked in war with the rest of the states (the Union). In 1862, with the war raging, President Lincoln declared all the slaves in the rebel states to be free as of January 1, 1863. It didn't do them much good, since their masters weren't taking orders from Lincoln anyway. But the proclamation did encourage more black men to enlist and fight. All in all, some 180,000 black soldiers served in the Union Army, and about a third were dead or missing by the end of the war.

In 1865, after devastating slaughter and destruction, the southern states finally surrendered. Before the year was out, slavery had been outlawed throughout the United States. The shameful story had finally come to an end.

One ironic twist in the final chapter of slavery in North America took place in Ontario. For some thirty years, the American government had deplored the Canadian policy toward slaves. Now, the administration of President Lincoln looked to Ontario for

This cheerful young woman is Edna Buckingham, employed by a family in Ancaster in 1915. It was a new century with a new set of worries; women were taking on more jobs, as men went off to Europe to fight the first world war.

guidance in how to help American ex-slaves – both the newly emancipated and the soon to be emancipated – build a new life.

During the summer of 1863, Samuel Gridley Howe and his colleagues were traveling throughout Ontario gathering material for their report on the progress of the blacks there. It had been argued that this information would be of little use, because people who had successfully escaped must be superior to those who had remained in slavery. This superiority, so the argument went, was proven by the ingenuity and courage they had displayed in making their escape.

The American commissioners rejected that argument. They concluded in their report that:

> No, the refugees in Canada earn a living and gather property; they marry and respect women; they build churches, and send their children to schools; they improve in manners and morals, – not because they are "picked men", but simply because they are free men.

12

Tracing Their Footsteps Today

This book was produced on behalf of two organizations working to preserve and promote black history: the Central Ontario Network for Black History, and the African Canadian Heritage Network. To contact the websites of the members of these organizations, please visit *www.underground-railroad.ca*.

For a more vivid and personal reminder of this history, we invite you to come and see our historic sites, which are listed on the following pages. Photographs of the sites below are accompanied by the words of some of those people who, more than a century and a half ago, played their parts in the extraordinary story of the Underground Railroad.

Uncle Tom's Cabin Historic Site, Dresden

After his dramatic adventures, Josiah Henson lived out his life in this handsome cabin in Dresden, site of the Dawn Settlement, until his death in 1883, at the age of ninety-four. The site includes original buildings and artifacts.

   In her introduction to Henson's autobiography, in 1876, Harriet Beecher Stowe paid him this tribute:

> The numerous friends of the author of this work will need no greater recommendation than his name to make it welcome. Among all the singular and interesting records to which the institution of American slavery has given rise, we know of none more striking, more characteristic and instructive, than that of JOSIAH HENSON.

Chatham-Kent Black Historical Society; Heritage Room at the WISH Centre, Chatham

The Heritage Room at the WISH community center pays tribute to the history of those who escaped slavery through a collection of artifacts, an extensive research collection, and genealogical material.

   A "John Brown Convention" was held

in Chatham in 1858. The prevailing sense of resolution was described by an unnamed participant:

> There was scant ceremony at these proceedings by these earnest men. They were of two colors but one mind and all were equal in degree and station here. No civic address to this Canadian town; no beat of drums; no firing of guns was heard. The place was rude and unadorned, yet the object of this little parliament was the freedom of four million slaves.

North American Black Historical Museum and Cultural Centre, Amherstburg

Amherstburg's location on the Detroit River made the town a major terminus of the Underground Railroad. The museum has artifacts, documents, and newspaper clippings of the time. William Wells Brown recorded his impressions of the community in 1861:

> At the entrance to the Detroit river, and 18 miles below Windsor, lies the village of Amherstburg, with a population of 2,200, of whom 400 are colored. This is one of the oldest

towns in this section of Canada. . . . Lying so near to Detroit, Amherstburg has long been one of the principal receiving depots of fugitives escaping by the Underground Railroad from the South. The colored population here seem to be in comfortable circumstances, most of them occupying their own dwellings, and appear to get ready employment. The Baptist Church is a neat building, capable of seating 400 persons, and has 150 members. . . . The Methodists have a small church and are erecting a new one, which they expect to occupy during the next year. . . .

Buxton National Historic Site & Museum, North Buxton

In the years preceding slavery's end, the Elgin Settlement at Buxton had about two thousand inhabitants. Although many returned to the United States after slavery was abolished, descendants of the settlers still live in the area. Some of them operate this museum, preserving the history of harder times.

Samuel Gridley Howe had high praise for Buxton in 1863, when he was studying the condition of former slaves for his report to the American government:

> Buxton is certainly a very interesting place. Sixteen years ago it was a wilderness. Now, good highways are laid out in all directions through the forest, and by their side are about two hundred cottages, all looking neat and comfortable. Around each one is a cleared space, which is well cultivated. There are

signs of industry, and thrift, and comfort, everywhere: signs of intemperance, of idleness, of want, nowhere.

Most interesting of all are the inhabitants. Twenty years ago, most of them were slaves, who owned nothing, not even their children. Now they own themselves; they own their houses and farms; and they have their wives and their children about them. They have the great essentials for human happiness; something to love, something to do, and something to hope for.

Sandwich Baptist Church, Windsor

This fine chapel, built in 1851, is one of the oldest black Baptist churches surviving from the days of the Underground Railroad. The church is still in use, and visitors are welcome to attend services.

The church was just ten years old when the Reverend William Troy paid a visit. Born in Virginia to a free mulatto mother and a slave father, Troy moved to Ontario in 1851 and

served as a Baptist minister in Amherstburg and later in
Windsor. In 1861 he published *Hairbreadth Escapes from Slavery
to Freedom*, including his own narrative and the stories of several
others who had escaped to Canada:

> Windsor is a town of three thousand inhabitants. Of these,
> eight hundred are coloured settlers from various portions of
> the Southern States of America. The town of Sandwich nearly
> joins Windsor; and it is thought that they will eventually be
> one place. In Sandwich there are about five hundred fugitive
> slaves. Adjacent to both these towns there are large numbers
> of fugitives, mostly engaged in farming. There are a few
> mechanics among them, – such as carpenters and joiners,
> bricklayers, masons, plasterers, and boot and shoe makers. In
> the settlements which I have visited there is every appearance
> of industry. Indeed, I look forward to the not far distant day
> when much, very much, will there be realised from moral and
> intellectual enterprises.

Stewart Memorial Church, Hamilton

For many fugitives, anywhere near the Detroit or Niagara River was uncomfortably close to the U.S. border, and the tricks and deceits of the slave-catchers. They felt safer in Hamilton. This BME church was acquired in 1879 by a congregation that dated back to the 1830s. It is still in use today.

Anthony Brown wrote a reassuring letter from Hamilton in 1856, sending messages to loved ones at home:

> We have spent quite an agreeable winter. . . . now we are all safe in Hamilton, I wish to call you to your promise, if convenient to write to Norfolk, Va. For me to let my wife Mary Ellen Brown, know where I am, and my brothers wife Elikzenzer Brown, as we have never heard a word from them since we left. Tell them that we found our homes and situation in Canada much better than we expected. Tell them not to think hard of us, we was bound to flee from the wrath to come, tell them we live in the hopes of meeting them once more this side of the grave. . . .

Mildred Mahoney Doll's House – Bertie Hall, Fort Erie

Stations of the Underground Railroad could be as humble as a potato cellar, or as grand as this mansion, Bertie Hall. The building is right on the Niagara River, so runaways still had to hide or they might be snatched back illegally by the slave-hunters who lay in wait. The house was said to have a secret tunnel leading to the riverbank, so that fugitives could slip inside without being spotted by hostile eyes. The building is now home to a dollhouse collection; the basement features sparse furnishings and a stirring collection of artifacts, as well as a hidden room, all lending a feeling of what it must have been like to escape on the Underground Railroad.

Josiah Henson's autobiography describes his first landing in Canada, near Fort Erie:

When I got on the Canada side, on the morning of the 28th of October, 1830, my first impulse was to throw myself on the ground, and giving way to the riotous exultation of my feelings, to execute sundry antics which excited the astonishment of those who were looking on. A gentleman of the neighborhood, Colonel Warren, who happened to be present, thought I was in a fit, and as he inquired what was the matter with the poor fellow, I jumped up and told him I was free. . . .

Nathaniel Dett Memorial Chapel, British Methodist Episcopal Church & Norval Johnson Library, Niagara Falls

This chapel was built in 1836, in Niagara Falls; it was later raised onto logs and rolled to a better location. It is still in use, both as a spiritual center and as a library of the heritage of one of Ontario's oldest black communities.

Frances Ellen Watkins Harper, one of the leading black poets and anti-slavery lecturers in the nineteenth century, traveled extensively on speaking tours. She wrote passionately about Niagara Falls in 1856:

> I have seen the ocean singing its wild chorus of sounding waves, and ecstasy has thrilled upon the living chords of my heart. I have since then seen the rainbow-crowned Niagara chanting the choral hymn of Omnipotence, girdled with grandeur, and robed with glory; but none of these things have melted me as the first sight of Free Land. . . . The first view of the ocean may fill you with strange delight. Niagara – the great, the glorious Niagara – may hush your spirit with its ceaseless thunder; it may charm you with its robe of crested spray and rainbow crown; but the land of Freedom was a lesson of deeper significance than foaming waves or towering mounts.

St. Catharines Museum at the Welland Canal Centre, St. Catharines

In 1849, when the second Welland Canal was being built, there was trouble between different factions of Irish laborers working on the project. A corps of black militia, the "Coloured Corps," was called out to keep the peace.

Seven years later, Benjamin Drew – the Boston abolitionist who published the personal narratives of fugitive slaves in his book *The Refugee* – expressed his thoughts about St. Catharines:

Refuge! Refuge for the oppressed! Refuge for the Americans escaping from abuse and cruel bondage in their native land! Refuge for my countrymen from the lash of the overseer, from the hounds and guns of southern man-hunters, from the clutches of northern marshals and commissioners! Rest! Rest for the hunted slave! Rest for the travel-soiled and foot-sore fugitive.

Refuge and Rest! These are the first ideas which arise in my mind in connection with the town of St. Catharines.

Salem Chapel, British Methodist Episcopal Church, St. Catharines

The black community first built a log chapel in St. Catharines, but in 1855 they replaced it with this graceful building. Inside, a three-sided balcony provided seating for a large congregation. Harriet Tubman is believed to have worshipped here, as did some of the people she led to safety. The church is still in use, and visitors are welcome.

James Massey had barely reached the safety of St. Catharines, in 1857, when he wrote these poignant words to the wife and family he had left behind:

I take this opportunity to inform you that I have arrived in St. Catharines this evening. After a journey of two weeks, and now find myself on free ground and wish that you was here with me. . . . I cannot tell how I come, for I was sometime on the earth and sometime under the earth. Do not be afraid to come, but start and keep trying. . . . Tell father and mother that I am safe and hope that they will not mourn after me. I shall ever remember them. No more at present, but yours in body and mind. And if we not meet on earth, I hope we shall meet in heaven. Your husband. Good night.

The Griffin House, Ancaster

This is the house of Enerals and Priscilla Griffin, a black couple who established a family farm near Ancaster in 1834. Their head-stones may be seen nearby, at St. Andrew's Presbyterian Church.

Six years before the Griffins arrived, members of the black community of Ancaster had published a petition in the *Ancaster Gazette*, explaining their needs in the third person:

One of the many, and perhaps the greatest disadvantage under which they labour, is the want of means of educating their children – which desirable object they fondly cherish the hopes of being able to accomplish, should they be formed

into a settlement, where they could combine and unite their means and exertions for so laudable a purpose as that of securing to their posterity the means of obtaining a moral and religious education, with all its happy consequences.

We hope you'll come and see all these sites, which convey the reality of the Underground Railroad more strikingly than any words can.

Also visit these friends and colleagues at our sister sites, who are likewise dedicated to preserving the black history of Ontario:

Sheffield Park Black History and Cultural Museum, Collingwood

John Freeman Walls Historic Site and Underground Railroad Museum, Puce

Fort Malden National Historic Site, Amherstburg

Fort George, Niagara-on-the-Lake

Oakville Museum at Erchless Estate, Oakville

Grey County Museum, Owen Sound

Ontario Black History Society, Toronto

Timeline

1501 Portuguese explorers enslave fifty native men and women in Labrador or Newfoundland.

1608 Mathieu de Costa is described as a "negro servant" of the governor of the French colony of Port-Royal, in what is now Nova Scotia.

1632 Oliver Le Jeune is the first black to appear in records as being brought directly from Africa and sold as a slave in New France.

1783 The American Revolution ends; United Empire Loyalists, both white and black, move to Canada – some accompanied by their slaves.

1793 Upper Canada's first legislature passes a law prohibiting the importation of more slaves, and decreeing the eventual emancipation of slaves born after that date.

The first Fugitive Slave Act is passed in the United States, mandating the return of runaway slaves.

1807 The British Parliament abolishes the slave trade.

1808 The U.S. Congress passes a law prohibiting the importation of slaves.

1812-1814 Britain and the United States fight the War of 1812. Companies of black soldiers take part in several battles.

1819 Upper Canada offers land in Simcoe County to black veterans of the War of 1812.

1828 The first African Methodist Episcopal Church (AME) in Ontario is built, in Amherstburg.

1829 Enforcement of punitive "Black Law" in Ohio leads refugees to form the Wilberforce Settlement, near present-day Lucan.

1831 William Lloyd Garrison begins publishing an anti-slavery newspaper, *The Liberator*.

1832 The Nat Turner Rebellion (a slave revolt in Virginia) results in more oppressive laws being imposed on blacks.

1833 Upper Canada refuses to extradite fugitive slaves Thornton and Lucie Blackburn, rescued by a mob in Detroit, back to the United States.

1834 The Emancipation Act, passed in 1833 (effective August 1, 1834), abolishes slavery throughout the British Empire, including Canada.

1837 Blacks from across Upper Canada join the "Coloured Corps" to defeat the Rebellion of 1837.

1838 Prompted by the case of Jesse Happy, a slave who escaped to Canada, the British government declares that a slave extradition request from the U.S. must show evidence that the person committed a crime recognized in Canada.

1840 A colored company of militia rescues two slaves from their master, who is visiting Niagara Falls.

1842 The Dawn Settlement, surrounding the British North American Institute, is founded near Dresden by Josiah Henson and Hiram Wilson.

1844 Levi Coffin, one of the most famous Underground Railroad conductors, visits Canada West to observe the progress of fugitive slaves, some of whom he aided in escaping.

1847 Frederick Douglass begins publication of the anti-slavery newspaper *North Star*.

1849 The Elgin Settlement and Buxton Mission is founded as a refuge for fugitive slaves.

1850 The passing of the second Fugitive Slave Act in the United States results in a flood of slaves and free blacks to the safety of Canada.

The Common School Act requires blacks in Ontario to attend separate schools where they exist.

1851 Henry and Mary Bibb begin publishing *The Voice of the Fugitive,* the first Canadian anti-slavery newspaper aimed at a black audience.

The Refugee Home Society is founded by Michigan and Canadian abolitionists, to establish a settlement near Windsor.

The Anti-Slavery Society of Canada, composed of whites and blacks, is founded in Toronto and spreads to other areas of Ontario.

The North American Convention at St. Lawrence Hall in Toronto draws anti-slavery leaders from across the U.S. and Canada West, to discuss emigration and other issues.

Harriet Tubman moves to St. Catharines and makes it the center of her anti-slavery activities for the next seven years.

1852 *Uncle Tom's Cabin*, by Harriet Beecher Stowe, brings international attention to the horrors of slavery.

1853 Mary Ann Shadd begins publishing *Provincial Freeman*, an anti-slavery newspaper, in Windsor. The paper is later published in Toronto and Chatham.

1856 The British Methodist Episcopal Church (BME) of Canada, eventually composed of churches across Ontario and in Michigan and Indiana, separates from the AME Church at a convention in Chatham. The name change is partly an expression of gratitude for the freedom found in the British colony.

The Amherstburg Baptist Association and Canadian Anti-Slavery Baptist Association unite, bringing together churches from across Ontario and Michigan.

Benjamin Drew publishes *The Refugee: or the Narratives of Fugitive Slaves in Canada*, recording interviews with blacks across Ontario.

1858 A crowd of both blacks and whites storms a train in Chatham and rescues a boy who is being kidnapped to be sold into slavery in the U.S.

John Brown holds a convention in Chatham to lay plans for the overthrow of slavery, and to adopt a constitution for a government of a proposed black homeland within North America.

1859 John Brown leads a raid on a weapons arsenal at Harper's Ferry, Virginia. Osborne Anderson from Chatham is among the freedom-fighters.

1860 The U.S. fails in its attempt to have Canada extradite John Anderson, from the Brantford area, who seven years earlier killed a man in Missouri who was trying to prevent his escape.

1861 Many Canadian blacks emigrate to Haiti as part of a larger settlement movement.

The American Civil War begins.

1863 The U.S. Emancipation Proclamation takes effect on January 1, declaring freedom for slaves in the rebelling territories.

The U.S. Freedmen's Inquiry Commission, led by Samuel Gridley Howe, tours black settlements throughout Ontario, preparing recommendations to assist U.S. plans for the transition from slavery to freedom.

Black soldiers are allowed to join the Union Army, and blacks from Canada flood to enlist. Many Canadians participate in that year's battle at Fort Wagner, in South Carolina (recently immortalized in the movie *Glory*), as members of the 54th Massachusetts (Colored) Regiment.

1865 The American Civil War ends. President Lincoln is assassinated. Slavery in North America finally comes to an end.

Acknowledgments

This book is sponsored by eleven of Ontario's historic sites, members of the African Canadian Heritage Network and the Central Ontario Network for Black History. The tourism departments of Windsor-Essex, Chatham-Kent, and NETCORP in Niagara, as well as the provincial Ministry of Tourism and Culture, and Parks Canada, are constant supporters of our work.

Supporters come from many, sometimes unexpected places. Among them are Gail Lord, of Lord Cultural Resources, based in Toronto, and Kathy Lowinger, of Tundra Books, who together have been responsible for giving our network of Underground Railroad sites the opportunity to share some of their stories, through the publication of this book.

There are many people to thank for sharing their passion and expertise on this subject. It has been my pleasure to have the opportunity to be in their company. A special word of thanks to my friend Joyce Middleton, to my wife, Shannon, and to my eldest son, Christopher, for their proofreading and their suggestions on the text. And a particular expression of appreciation to this book's editor, Gena Gorrell.

B.P.

Suggested Reading

Bradford, Sarah. *Scenes in the Life of Harriet Tubman.* Auburn, NY: W.J. Moses, 1879.

Brode, Patrick. *The Odyssey of John Anderson.* Toronto, ON: University of Toronto Press, 1989.

Coffin, Levi. *Reminiscences of Levi Coffin.* Cincinnati, OH: Robert Clark, 1880.

Drew, Benjamin. *The Refugee: or the Narratives of Fugitive Slaves in Canada.* Boston, MA: John Jewett, 1856.

Forbes, Ella. *But We Have No Country: The 1851 Christiana, Pennsylvania Resistance.* Cherry Hill, NJ: Africana Homestead Legacy Publishers, 1998.

French, Gary. *Men of Colour: An Historical Account of the Black Settlement on Wilberforce Street in Oro Township, Simcoe County, Ontario 1819–1949.* Stroud, ON: Kaste Books, 1978.

Gara, Larry. *The Liberty Line: The Legend of the Underground Railroad.* Lexington, KY: University of Kentucky Press, 1961.

Hill, Daniel G. *The Freedom-Seekers: Blacks in Early Canada.* Agincourt, ON: Book Society of Canada, 1981.

Howe, Samuel Gridley, *et al. Howe: Report to the Freedmen's Inquiry Commission 1864: The Refugees from Slavery in Canada West.* Reprinted by Arno Press and the *New York Times,* New York, NY, 1969.

Meyler, Peter. *Broken Shackles: Old Man Henson from Slavery to Freedom*. Toronto, ON: Natural Heritage, 2001.

Meyler, Peter, and David Meyler. *A Stolen Life: Searching for Richard Pierpont*. Toronto, ON: Natural Heritage, 1999.

Middleton, Joyce, *et al. Something to Hope for: The Story of the Fugitive Slave Settlement, Buxton, Canada West*. North Buxton, ON: Buxton National Historic Site & Museum, 2000.

Mitchell, Rev. W.M. *The Under-Ground Railroad*. Westport, CT: Negro Universities Press, 1860 (reprinted 1970).

Pease, Jane, and William Pease. *They Who Would Be Free: Blacks' Search for Freedom, 1830–1861*. Urbana and Chicago, IL: University of Illinois Press, 1990.

Power, Michael, and Nancy Butler. *Slavery and Freedom in Niagara*. Niagara-on-the-Lake, ON: Niagara Historical Society, 1993, 2000.

Rhodes, Jane. *Mary Ann Shadd Cary: The Black Press and Protest in the Nineteenth Century*. Bloomington and Indianapolis, IN: Indiana University Press, 1998.

Ripley, C. Peter, *et al. Black Abolitionist Papers, Volume II: Canada, 1830–1865*. Chapel Hill, NC: University of North Carolina Press, 1986.

Robbins, Arlie. *Legacy to Buxton*. North Buxton, ON: Arlie and Laverne Robbins, 1983.

Robinson, Gwendolyn, and John Robinson. *Seek the Truth: A Story of Chatham's Black Community*. Chatham, ON, 1986.

Severance, Frank. *Old Trails on the Niagara Frontier*. Cleveland, OH: Burrows Brothers, 1903.

Shadd, Adrienne, Afua Cooper, and Karolyn Smardz-Frost. *The Underground Railroad: Next Stop Toronto!* Toronto, ON: Natural Heritage, 2002.

Shreve, Dorothy S. *The AfriCanadian Church: A Stabilizer*. Jordan Station, ON: Paideia, 1983.

Siebert, Wilbur H. *The Underground Railroad: From Slavery to Freedom*. London, England: Macmillan, 1898. Reprinted by Arno Press and the *New York Times*, New York, NY, 1963.

Simpson, Donald. *Under the North Star*. Toronto, ON: Harriet Tubman Resource Centre, York University, 2003.

Still, William. *The Underground Railroad*. 1871. Reprinted by Johnson Publishing. Chicago, IL, 1970.

Stouffer, Allen P. *The Light of Nature and the Law of God: Antislavery in Ontario 1833–1877*. Montreal, QC, Kingston, London, ON.: McGill-Queen's University Press, 1992.

Stowe, Harriet Beecher. *A Key to Uncle Tom's Cabin*. Boston, MA: John P. Jewett, 1853.

Thomas, Owen. *Niagara's Freedom Trail: A Guide to African-Canadian History of the Niagara Peninsula*. Region of Niagara Tourist Council, 1995.

Ullman, Victor. *Look to the North Star: A Life of William King*. Boston, MA: Beacon, 1969.

Winks, Robin W. *The Blacks in Canada: A History*. Montreal, QC, Kingston, London, ON: McGill-Queen's University Press. Reprinted 1997.

Source Notes

Bibliographic information is given where a book is first referred to, unless the book is included in the list Suggested Reading. Each chapter epigraph is drawn from a quotation later in the chapter.

Chapter 1: Human Cargo, Human Wares

The story of Oliver Le Jeune is drawn from *The Blacks in Canada*, by Winks. The remark from the Marquis De Vaudreuil is from a letter to Commandant Bellestre, cited in *The Windsor Border Region*, edited by Ernest J. Lajeunesse (Toronto, ON: University of Toronto Press, 1960). The story of Margaret Kleine is drawn from *The Trail of the Black Walnut*, by G. Elmore Reaman (Toronto, ON: McClelland and Stewart, 1959) and *Wilderness Christians: The Moravian Mission to the Delaware Indians*, by Elma E. Gray (New York, NY: Athenaeum, 1973). The story of Sarah Cole is drawn from "The Slave in Canada," by William R. Riddell, in *The Journal of Negro History*, Vol. 5, No. 3 (July 1920). The Crooks' advertisement is cited in "Slave Days in Canada," a paper presented to the Women's Canadian Historical Society of Toronto by Mrs. W. T. Hallam, in April 1919 (copy in author's possession).

Chapter 2: Oppression and Injustice

The advertisements placed by Russell and Field and the will of Antoine Louis Descompte are cited in "The Slave in Canada," by Riddell. John Baker's story is cited in *Lunenburgh, or the Old Eastern District*, published by J.F. Pringle, Judge, County Court, in 1890; my thanks to Bill Martin of Thunder Bay for making this publication available on the

Internet. Josiah Cutten's story appears in the John Askin Papers, Vol. 1, edited by Milo M. Quaife, published by the Detroit Library Commission, 1928. The information on the gibbet comes from *The Township of Sandwich Past and Present*, by Frederick Neal (Windsor, ON: Record Printing, 1909).

Chapter 3: Cruelty and Kindness

General Murray's quote is cited in "The Slave in Canada," by Riddell. The article beginning "On the faithfulness" was by Watson H. Smith and appeared in the Nova Scotia Historical Society Records, Vol. 10; cited in *National Problems of Canada: The Negro in Canada*, by Ida Greaves (Orillia, ON: Packet Times, undated, for McGill University, Montreal, QC). The story about Mott is drawn from "The Slave in Canada," by Riddell. Gray's letter is cited in the John Askin Papers, Vol. 1. The Moravian service is mentioned in *Wilderness Christians: The Moravian Mission to the Delaware Indians*, by Gray. James Girty's will appears in *History of the Girtys*, by Consul Willshire Butterfield, reprinted by Long's College Book Co., Columbus, OH (1950).

Chapter 4: Turbulent Times

The description of Elliott's estate is from *The Windsor Border Region*, edited by Lajeunesse. Bill's story is drawn from *The Simcoe Papers*, Vol. 4, collected and edited by Brig. Gen. E.A. Cruikshank (Toronto, ON: Ontario Historical Society, 1926), and "The Slave in Canada," by Riddell. Askin's letters appear in the John Askin Papers, Vol. 2. The Amy Ford Martin quote is from *Howe: Report to the Freedmen's Inquiry Commission 1864*, referred to hereafter as the Howe report.

Chapter 5: Emancipation throughout the Empire

Smith's letter is from *The Simcoe Papers*, Vol 1. Jefferson's objection and the British response are found in *The Simcoe Papers*, Vol. 2 and 3 respectively; the quote "every slave like every horse" appears in a letter from John Jay to Edmund Randolph, Sept. 13, 1794. Richard Pierpont's story is told in *A Stolen Life*, by Meyler and Meyler. The Lundy quote is from *The Diary of Benjamin Lundy*, by Fred Landon, found in the Ontario Historical Society papers, Vol. 19. The material on the O'Briens is drawn from *The Journals of Mary O'Brien 1828–1838*, edited by Audrey

Saunders Miller (Toronto, ON: Macmillan, 1968). Loguen's declaration
(photo caption) is from *The Rev. J.W. Loguen As a Slave and As a
Freeman* (Syracuse, NY: J.G.K. Truair, 1859). The quote "We are here
met" is from *The Bytown Gazette and Ottawa Advertiser*, Aug. 21, 1839.

Chapter 6: Setting Out for the Unknown

The Johnson quote is from *Africa for Christ: Twenty-Eight Years a Slave*,
by Rev. Thomas L. Johnson (London, England: Alexander and
Shepheard, no date). The Lindsey quote is from the Howe report. The
Webb quote is from "The Model Negro Colony in Kent," by G.C.
Porter, an undated manuscript in the Victor Ullman Collection at
Buxton National Historic Site & Museum. The horror stories of cut-off
heads and hangings are drawn from *Old Trails on the Niagara Frontier*,
by Severance. The stories of Alfred Jones, John Francis, Robert Nelson,
and Edward Hicks are drawn from *The Refugee*, by Drew. The *Niagara
Mail* article was published on Aug. 10, 1853. The Lyford quote is from a
letter written to Wilbur Siebert on March 27, 1896, found in the Wilbur
Siebert Papers at the Houghton Library of Harvard University and
quoted in *The Liberty Line*, by Gara.

Chapter 7: The Kindness of Strangers

Betsey Robinson's story is drawn from *Old Trails on the Niagara
Frontier*, by Severance. The Morehead quote is from *The Refugee*, by
Drew. Harrison Webb's story is drawn from "The Model Negro Colony
in Kent," by Porter. The quotes from Margaret Cadham (photo
caption) appear in a letter supplied by Wilma Morrison of the Norval
Johnson Heritage Library, at Nathaniel Dett BME Church, Niagara
Falls, ON. The George Washington remark appears in a letter of April
12, 1786, cited in *Eyewitness: The Negro in American History*, by William
Loren Katz (New York, NY: Pitman, 1972). *Narrative of the Life of J.D.
Green* was published in Huddersfield, England, in 1864, by Henry
Fielding. *Narrative of William W. Brown* was published in Boston, MA,
in 1847, by the Anti-Slavery Office.

Chapter 8: Some Names Not Forgotten

The remarks on John Fairfield are drawn partly from *A Woman's Life-
Work: Labours and Experiences of Laura S. Haviland*, by Laura Haviland

(Cincinnati, OH: Walden & Stowe, 1882), and *Reminiscences of Levi Coffin*, by Coffin. The story of Solomon Northup and Samuel Bass is drawn from Northup's biography, *Twelve Years a Slave* (Philadelphia, PA: Columbia, 1890). Birney's remarks are from a letter of Feb. 27, 1837, in *Letters of James Gillespie Birney*, edited by Dwight L. Diamond (New York, NY: Appleton-Century, 1938), found on *www.marcusgarvey.com*). *The Life of Josiah Henson, Formerly a Slave, Now an Inhabitant of Canada, As Narrated by Himself*, was first published in 1849, by A. D. Phelps of Boston, MA. The story of John Mason is draw from *The Under-Ground Railroad*, by Mitchell. Frederick Douglass's autobiography, *Life and Times of Frederick Douglass*, was published in 1881 by Park, in Hartford, CT. Still's book, *The Underground Railroad*, was published in 1871 in Philadelphia, reprinted in 1970 by Johnson in Chicago. The story of Dick Sims is drawn from the unpublished autobiography of the Rev. William King, at Buxton National Historic Site & Museum. Quotes about Tubman from Smith, Tubman, Brown, and Douglass are drawn from *Scenes in the Life of Harriet Tubman*, by Bradford.

Chapter 9: Desperate Measures
The Blackburns' story is drawn from "Fugitive Slaves Thornton & Lucie Blackburn and the Rise of Black Resistance in Detroit and Toronto, 1833-1853," a 2003 doctoral thesis by Karolyn Smardz-Frost at the University of Waterloo, ON. The Hackett story is drawn partially from the *Chatham Journal*, Sept. 11, 1841. The Crosswhites' story is drawn partially from Sarah Crosswhite's deposition in the U.S. National Archives (Great Lakes Region, Chicago, Record Group 21). The Glover story is drawn from *The Underground Railroad*, by Siebert. The material regarding Reverend King and Daniel Ducket is drawn from the autobiography of the Rev. William King, in the King Papers at the National Archives of Canada. The Sanford story is drawn from *Hairbreadth Escapes from Slavery to Freedom*, by the Rev. William Troy (Manchester, England: W. Bremner, 1861). The story of the siblings dressed as sailors is drawn from *Sketches in the History of the Underground Railroad*, by Eber M. Pettit (Fredonia, NY: McKinstry & Son, 1879). The story of Daniel Payne is drawn from *A Woman's Life-Work*, by Haviland. The story of the Babys is drawn from *Souvenirs of Our Past*, by William Lewis Baby (Windsor, ON: 1896). Anna Jameson's

observations were published in two volumes under the title *Winter Studies and Summer Rambles in Canada* (New York, NY: Wiley and Putnam, 1839).

Chapter 10: Hard Times in a Hard Land
The request for a separate parcel of property is drawn from *Loyalist Mosaic: A Multi-Ethnic Heritage*, by Joan Magee (Toronto, ON: Dundurn, 1984). The material on John Prince is drawn from *John Prince*, by Douglas. Ward's letter to *The Voice of the Fugitive* appeared in the issue of Nov. 5, 1851. The petition to the synod appears in the King Papers, as do the James Thompson quotes. *Roughing It in the Bush* was republished in Toronto by McClelland & Stewart in 1962. Murray's observation appears in *Letters from the United States, Cuba and Canada*, by Amelia Murray (New York, NY: G.P. Putnam, 1856). The story of the Willis children is drawn from *The Recollections of Edwin Bassett Jones*, published by his daughter Grace Jones Morgan in 1974, also drawn from the author's collection. The description of the Niagara schoolhouse (photo caption) is by Mary Ann Guillan, reported in "Slave Rescue in Niagara, Sixty Years Ago," by Janet Carnochan, in a Niagara Historical Society pamphlet, cited in *Slavery and Freedom in Niagara*, by Power and Butler. The quote from Chambers is from American Missionary Association records housed at Tulane University, LA (microfilm at Robarts Library, University of Toronto). The Mason story is found in *Old Trails on the Niagara Frontier*, by Severance. The story of Parker Joyner is also drawn from American Missionary Association records (Sept. 14, 1863). Miller's quote appears in *The Refugee*, by Drew. A copy of Field's will is in the author's collection. The caption about Jim Henson is based on information from *Broken Shackles*, by Meyler. The Baumont interview was carried out in Clark County, Ohio, on March 19, 1927, and is found in a wonderful website hosted by the Ohio Historical Society at *www.ohio-history.org*. Note that the language has been changed from the original, stereotypical slang dialect.

Chapter 11: Learning to Live in Liberty
Slight's remark is from his diary, at the United Church Archives, Toronto. The Tubman quote is from *The Refugee*, by Drew. King's

comments are from his autobiography. The ship captain's remarks are from *Sketches in the History of the Underground Railroad*, by Pettit. Some information about the Refugee Home Society is drawn from a letter written from Rochester, Essex County, by AMA missionary David Hotchkiss on May 12, 1860, and from *The Bark Covered House, or Back in the Woods Again*, by William Nowlin (Detroit, 1876). *A Plea for Emigration; or, Notes from Canada West* was published by George W. Pattison in Detroit, in 1852. The story of the Smiths appeared in *The Voice of the Fugitive*, over the first six months of 1852, based on Henry Bibb's interviews of James Smith.

Chapter 12: Tracing Their Footsteps Today

Henson's autobiography is *The Life of Josiah Henson, Formerly a Slave*. The quote from the John Brown Convention appears in the Hunton Collection in the Chatham-Kent Black Historical Society archives. William Wells Brown's remarks are drawn from his article "The Colored People of Canada," originally written for the Haytian Emigration Bureau in 1861 and reprinted in *The Black Abolitionist Papers* (Vol. 2), by Ridley. Howe's description appears in the Howe report. Troy's remarks appear in *Hairbreadth Escapes*. Anthony Brown's letter, and the remarks of Watkins Harper and Massey, appear in *The Underground Railroad*, by Still; spelling and punctuation have been adjusted for clarity. Drew's remarks are drawn from *The Refugee*. The quote from the *Ancaster Gazette* is cited in the *Gazette and Religious Advocate* (Kingston, ON, July 25, 1828).

Picture Sources

Every reasonable effort has been made to trace the ownership of copyright materials. Any information allowing the publisher to correct a reference or credit in future will be welcomed. Pictures not attributed are from the author's collection. For space reasons the following abbreviations have been used:

AO	Archives of Ontario
BNHSM	Buxton National Historic Site & Museum
GCA	Grey County Archives, ON
LOC	Library of Congress (U.S.A.)
NAC	National Archives of Canada
NHSM	Niagara Historical Society and Museum, Niagara-on-the-Lake, ON
TPL	Toronto Public Library

Page v: courtesy BNHSM; vi: Mark Kulas, data courtesy Ontario's Underground Railroad Alliance; 2: courtesy Uncle Tom's Cabin Historic Site, Dresden, ON; 3: courtesy Chatham-Kent Black Historical Society; 5: TPL; 7: *Négrier poursuivi*, © Musée national de la marine, Paris, France; 9: "The land of the free and the home of the braves [*sic*] (Slave market) (Charleston, SC)" by Henry Byam Martin, NAC, C-115001; 12: AO; 13: *top, Slave with Iron Muzzle*, courtesy Hill Collection of Pacific Voyages, University of California, San Diego, *bottom right*, courtesy BNHSM; 16: AO, S2076; 21: *top*, LOC, LC-USZ62-10476 (3-18), *bottom*, New York Historical Society, #38219; 23: courtesy Anita Toliver, Stewart Memorial Church; 27: courtesy BNHSM; 31: AO, C 281-0-0-0-8; 34:

Painting by John Wycliffe Lowes Forster, NAC, C-008111; 37 *top*: National Library of Canada, *bottom*, TPL; 38: courtesy NHSM, 984.5.142; 40: NAC, C-147912, C-147913; 41: NAC, RG 8 series 1, vol. 1702, reel C -3839, page 242; 43: from *The Rev. J.W. Loguen, as a Slave and as a Freeman: A Narrative of Real Life*, courtesy of the Divinity School Library, Duke University, Durham, NC; 50: *top*, LOC, LC-DIG-CW pbh-05089, *bottom*, AO, F-4356-0-0-0-43; 54: courtesy NHSM, 988.203; 55: LOC, LC-B8171-518 (4-4); 57: courtesy Ontario's Underground Railroad Alliance; 60-61: AO, Alvin D. McCurdy Collection, F-2076-16-1-1-2; 64: Norval Johnson Heritage Library, Nathaniel Dett Chapel; 71: *left*, TPL, *right*, courtesy Levi Coffin House Association and Waynet; 72: TPL; 74: courtesy Lenawee County Historical Museum, Adrian, MI; 78: LOC, Rare Books and Special Collections Division; 83: LOC, LC-USZ62-106337; 89: LOC, LC-USZ62-90750; 93: GCA; 96: courtesy Brooklyn Museum of Art; 97: courtesy NHSM, 984.5.117; 102: AO, Alvin D. McCurdy Collection, F-2076-16-3-4-22; 104: drawing by Owen Staples, courtesy of NHSM; 106: courtesy Amistad Research Center, Tulane University, LA; 107: Norval Johnson Heritage Library, Nathaniel Dett Chapel; 109: GCA; 113: AO, Alvin D. McCurdy Collection, F-2076-16-1-6-1-23; 115: courtesy Mr. & Mrs. Robert Schram, St. Catharines Museum, St. Catharines, ON; 117: TPL; 119: Grey County Museum; 122: NAC, C-029977; 125: photo by Andrew & Sandra Goss, Owen Sound, ON; 127: Hamilton Region Conservation Authority, Fieldcote Memorial Park and Museum and Griffin House; 138: courtesy Eva Salter

Index